Warmth Course

Fourteen lectures by

Rudolf Steiner

Stuttgart, March 1 - 14, 1920

MERCURY PRESS

This is the second Mercury Press edition of the
Warmth Course. It is a completely revised and emended translation of the
original translation from the German done by George Adams.

This revision was done by Alice Barton Wulsin and
Gerald F. Karnow, M.D. in accordance with the most recent German
edition, *Geisteswissenschaftliche Impulse zur Entwicklung der Physik,
Zweiter naturwissenschaftlicher Kurs,* Bibliographie-Nr. 321, published by
the Rudolf Steiner Nachlassverwaltung, Dornach, 1982. The editors of that
German edition were G.A. Balaster and A. Dollfus.

The introduction and notes of this edition are their work translated
by G.F. Karnow.

The drawings were done by Hedwig Frey
according to the original blackboard drawings done by Rudolf Steiner.

The cover was designed by Peter van Oordt.

All rights reserved
Copyright © 2022
by Mercury Press

ISBN: 978-1-957569-00-0

MERCURY PRESS
an imprint of SteinerBooks
PO Box 58, Hudson, NY 12534
www.steinerbooks.org

Contents

Introduction i
    G.A. Balaster and A. Dollfus

Lecture I
March 1, 1920 1

    Sensation of warmth and the thermometer. Achilles and the turtle. The tragedy of a thinking removed from perception. Atomism. Cosmic theories. Constitution of the sun: negative matter. The contrast between seeing colors and the sensation of warmth. Mechanical theory of heat. The irreversibility of organic and large inorganic processes; integration and differentiation in relationship to reality.

Lecture II
March 2, 1920 17

    Warmth expansion in one, two, and three dimensions. Ignoring higher potencies cancels out essentials. Individual coefficient of expansion of solid bodies and uniform expansion of gaseous bodies as symptoms. *Accademia del Cimento* at the transition to a more modern physics. A multitude of detailed observations compared with impoverished concepts. The irregular behavior of water. Cosmic forces in the physics of the Greeks and their later displacement into atoms.

Lecture III
March 3, 1920 31

    Cessation of temperature rise during melting and boiling. Disappearance of points into a higher dimension. Goethean physics. Temperature as fourth dimension for Crookes. Individual form of the solid body, pressure of the gas.

Lecture IV
March 4, 1920 43

    Relationship of pressure and volume in gases. The nature of warmth in connection to mechanical facts. The departure from three-dimensional space. The judgment: warmth transforms itself into work. Isolated sense organs for light and tone, the entire human being as sense organ for warmth and pressure. Conscious, passive conceptions filtered out of perceptions of the higher senses. Imperceptibility of the will as one proceeds inward and of electricity as one proceeds outward.

Lecture V
March 5, 1920 57

Higher conceptions and sense perception, mathematical conceptions and will. Bridging dualism. Memorizing a poem. Abstract thinking and imaginative thinking. Knowledge of space and time on the one hand, of mass on the other. Kant. Individual form of solid bodies and the surface level of fluids. Gas and cosmos. Water as the cardinal exception.

Lecture VI
March 6, 1920 71

Steam pressure. Melting of ice under pressure. Lowering of melting point in an alloy. Lines of fall of solid bodies and their surface levels; in liquids these are materially present. Solid bodies as picture of the fluid; fluid as picture of the gas; gas as picture of warmth.

Lecture VII
March 7, 1920 81

Melting of ice under pressure as picture of air. Discarding the essentiality from the concepts of modern natural science. Eduard von Hartmann. The significance of new research institutes. Heating water by work. Solid planet: gravity; aeriform planet: negative gravity; fluid planet: null sphere. Polyhedral structure, negative form, sphere or null sphere. Relations to solid, gaseous, fluid. Warmth night and warmth day.

Lecture VIII
March 8, 1920 93

Steam engine. Transformation of heat into work and the reverse. The two axioms of the theory of heat in Eduard von Hartmann. J. R. Mayer. The dispute about a "closed system" in the solid body. Schema of body states: shape in solid; densification-rarefaction in the gaseous; fluid in between; warmth between densification and rarefaction and between becoming material and becoming spiritual. The ordinary spectrum and Goethe's closed color circle. Comparison with the schema of the body states.

Lecture IX
March 9, 1920 107

Water wheel and steam engine. Achievement based on differences of level. Approaching the human being with physical phenomena. The path of J. R. Mayer. The regions of corporeality: one has its image in the other. Polarization figures. Densification-rarefaction and tone. Rainbow and secondary rainbow. In the usual spectrum something remains in the unknown. Earth rotation in relation to the physical realms.

Lecture X
March 10, 1920 120

Separation of heat effects from a light cylinder through alum. Passage of warmth through an ice lens. Warmth conduction. The conditions of corporeality and the human being. Structural force – conception; warmth – will. Negative matter in the human being. Suction effect vs. pressure effect.

Lecture XI
March 11, 1920 131

The red, blue and green parts of the spectrum. Separation of heat effects by alum, of chemical effects by aesculin, of light effects by iodine. The ordinary spectrum as the result of earthly forces. Comparison with the effects of the magnet. Darkening – illumination. Materialization-dematerialization. Warmth as intensive movement instead of extensive movement of atoms. Will and conceptions. Warmth at the border of pressure and suction effects. E. Mach concerning the limits of the energy law. Warmth as physical-spiritual vortex.

Lecture XII
March 12, 1920 143

Transparency. Warmth conduction equation. Expansion of the corresponding effects of the various parts of the spectrum. Positive, negative, imaginary numbers. Superimaginary numbers and bending the spectrum. Life's place in relation to inorganic nature.

Lecture XIII
March 13, 1920 155

Experiment with alum, iodine, aesculin. Warmth works in gas – light passes through without participation: image of image. Chemical effects in the liquid. Life effects in the solid are absent. Warmth as state of balance between the etheric and the ponderable-material. Physics of the past and the future. Null sphere as spatial border of contemporary physics. Entropy.

Lecture XIV
March 14, 1920 165

Effects are pure in the spectrum. Chemical effect – chemical processes; chemical effect – sound effects. Taking hold of the effect by the earth in one case, by the peripheral working in the other case. Ponderable and imponderable effects. Differences of level within one realm of reality and between different realms. Tone perception. Filling of space – emptying of space. Earth and planets. Cosmic effects are displaced into atoms. Tearing apart of space, lightning. Abstract conceptions – thinking in accord with reality. Public schools, preparatory schools, technological schools. Embryology, considered microscopically from the viewpoint of its cosmic starting points.

Notes 181

Introduction

G.A. Balaster and A. Dollfus
Editors of the Second German Edition
of The Warmth Course

Rudolf Steiner conducted both the second natural scientific course presented in this book and the first such course[1] (on light) in the Waldorf School in Stuttgart. Approximately the same small circle of people participated in both courses, primarily members of the faculty of the Waldorf School (a school guided by Rudolf Steiner's insights), as well as a few members of the Anthroposophical Society who had been trained in mathematics and natural science. It was possible for Rudolf Steiner to speak to them as individuals fundamentally acquainted with the impulses of his spiritual science. They had acquired their own judgments concerning the foundation and concrete steps of his activity and were themselves willing to work in the direction of these impulses. Publication of such lecture material could be subject to misunderstandings if the situation under which these lectures were given were not taken into consideration. They do not attempt to present a new physics, complete once and for all, but rather they seek to extend natural scientific points of view. The hope was that this would stimulate further research by individuals thoroughly trained in various special fields. What was thus given as a stimulus in a very specific circle of individualities is able to address itself through publication to anyone able to recognize a significance in the scientific direction indicated. This volume must be considered in the context of the complete edition of Rudolf Steiner's works out of which it originates. It is only a building block in the structure of the entire opus that, insofar as it comes to expression in the writings and lectures, can be considered as a totality.

Rudolf Steiner mentions in this course that he wishes to offer something to the teachers that would help them instruct their classes. It is quite clear, however, that what is required is not simply a matter of lecturing about physics in school; rather, as everywhere in Rudolf Steiner's work, what is necessary is to educate and train our thinking and approach to knowing. These must first be brought to an extended grasp of reality. In natural science, and especially in physics, Goethe demonstrated such a grasp of reality in his way. The physics taught today is certainly far removed from the Goethean approach, yet our contemporary situation is being remarkably illuminated by the fact that a few leading physicists today are developing a keen interest in Goethe's investigations, which had been ignored and neglected by scientists for one and a half centuries.

The "how" of the development offered in these lectures was certainly quite surprising for those who heard them in 1920. It is equally so for the reader today, and this for a very special reason. If an individual looks at the development of physics in the years after Rudolf Steiner's death and reads the twelfth lecture with sufficiently broad perspective, he is likely to be surprised at how the mathematical deliberations that may appear as a special episode in the totality of the course point precisely to the matters in which decisive events have since occurred in physics: the equation of the conduction of warmth with imaginary coefficients and the inclusion of superimaginary numbers in physics. The fact that this direction was taken in this course on the basis of entirely different relationships than was the case later in atomic physics opens a perspective pointing to the far wider significance of these steps than was understood until now. On the other hand, it also raises questions concerning the actual nature of this more modern atomic physics itself. At the end of the eleventh lecture, Rudolf Steiner states the following: "That modern physics does not develop this concept, this concept of negative matter, which is related to outer matter like suction to pressure, is the misfortune of modern physics." Now this sounds quite different to a contemporary physicist from the way it did to the physicists attending this course. However, the context out of which Rudolf Steiner speaks and the very different context in which atomic physics was led to the concept of antimatter prevents one from claiming that "negative matter" and "antimatter" are the same. Again the question arises of what the relationship is between the domain of reality that has arisen in atomic physics and the natural domains of reality developed in this course. Insight into this ought to become evident out of a real understanding of this course's progression compared with the path of atomic physics. In addition to what becomes clear regarding this question in this course, various aspects of an answer can be found scattered throughout Rudolf Steiner's entire work. An essential aspect is given in his 1911 lecture, "The Etherization of the Blood," in which, in addition to the physical and superphysical worlds, the subphysical world is characterized.

We can see, then, that at the time of the present publication of this course, the development of physics itself has contributed something to what these lectures were able to offer at the time they were given.

Some additional comments are necessary concerning the publication of this course. It is tremendously difficult to take shorthand notes in such a course, where experiments were conducted simultaneously with speaking and where notes were written and sketches drawn on the board. As a consequence, a completely faithful recapturing of the original presentation appears almost impossible. What made this task of publication even more difficult was that no stenographers' notes were available but only a copy compiled from stenographic notes. The work on this recent edition has shown that many apparently meaningless comments appeared in earlier texts because someone unfamiliar with the subject had deciphered the stenographic abbreviations. When speaking once about the publication of his natural scientific courses, Rudolf Steiner spoke of the notes as a "cabbage stew" that he would first have to correct so that it would have the appropriate meaning. He did not get to this task. It is certainly possible that in the present text there are still incorrect statements here and there, because the most significant task of the editors had to be to ensure that no really intended thought of the lecturer was altered – and certainly we are not dealing with customary thoughts here. In a late phase of the preparation for this volume, the editors had a number of copies of the first edition at their disposal, in which various readers of the course made suggestions for corrections. These ranged from isolated comments at specific points to thoroughly edited manuscripts. The editors have carefully evaluated many of these suggestions and used them freely. They owe the elucidation of many questionable sections to such assistance. There are also frequent instances where the present text returns to the words of the original copy, which had been modified in certain places in the first publication of the course, but without sufficient reason in our judgment.

Lecture I

Stuttgart,
March 1, 1920

The present course of lectures will offer a kind of continuation of the natural scientific studies given when I was last here. I will begin with a chapter of physics that can be particularly important in laying a foundation for a natural scientific worldview in general, namely the study of the relationships of heat in the world. Today I will try to lay out an introduction to show you how we can become aware of the significance of physical knowledge within a general worldview and how a foundation may thus be secured for a pedagogical impulse applicable to teaching natural science. Today we will therefore go as far as we can toward outlining a general introduction.

During the nineteenth century, the theory of heat, as it is called, took on a form that has given a great deal of support to a materialistic view of the world. This is due to the fact that when considering heat relationships it is very easy to turn one's gaze away from the real nature of heat, from its being, and to direct it to the mechanical phenomena arising from heat relationships.

Heat is known to us first through sensations described as cold, warm, lukewarm, and so on. We soon learn, however, that there appears to be something vague about these sensations, something subjective. This becomes clear through a simple experiment that anyone can make.

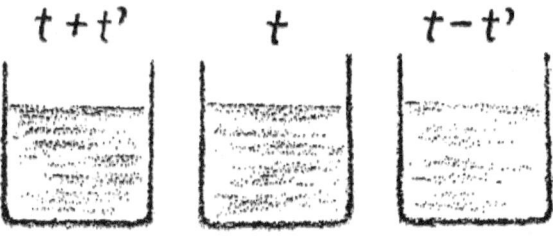

Imagine that here you have a vessel filled with water of a definite temperature, t; on the right of it you have another vessel filled with water of a temperature, *t-t'*, that is, of a temperature distinctly lower than the temperature in the first vessel.² In addition, you have a vessel filled with water at a temperature *t* + *t'*. If you now place your fingers in the two outer vessels, your sensations will indicate to you the heat conditions in these vessels. You can then plunge the fingers that have been in the outer vessels into the central vessel; you will see that the water in the central vessel will feel warm to the fingers that have been in the cooler water, while to the fingers that were in the warmer water, the water in the central vessel will feel cool. The same temperature, therefore, is subjectively experienced differently according to the temperature to which one has previously been exposed.

You all know that if you go into a cellar, it may feel different in the winter from the way it feels in summer. Even though the thermometer registers the same temperature, circumstances may be such that the cellar feels warm in the winter and cool in the summer. Indeed, the subjective experience of heat is not uniform, and it is necessary to set an objective standard for measuring the heat condition of any object or location. Here I do not need to go into the elementary phenomena or consider the elementary instruments used for measuring heat. I must assume that you are acquainted with them. I will simply say that when the temperature condition is measured with a thermometer, we have the feeling that since we measure the degree above or below zero, we are getting an objective temperature measurement. In our thinking we consider there to be a fundamental difference between this objective determination, in which we have no part, and the subjective determination, where the human being takes part in the experience.

For all that the nineteenth century has striven to attain, it may be said that this view of matter was, from a certain viewpoint, fruitful and justified by its results. We live in a time now, however, when attention must be paid to certain things in order to advance productively in one or another field of knowledge or practical life. Certain questions must arise out of science itself that are simply overlooked in conclusions such as those I have given. One question is this: is there a difference – a real, objective difference – between my organism's determination of temperature and that of a thermometer, or do I deceive myself for the sake of getting useful practical results when I take such a difference into account in my concepts? This whole course will be designed to show why such questions must be asked today. It will be my aim to proceed from fundamental questions to questions that are simply overlooked today in practical life because such matters have not been taken into account. You will see how they have been neglected in the area of technology. I would like to impress you with the fact that we have completely lost our attention to the real nature of heat under the influence of certain ideas to be described presently. Along with this loss, we have also lost the possibility of bringing the nature of heat into relation to the human organism itself, a relationship that must be established in certain areas of life.

I will begin with preliminary indications of how these things relate to the human organism. First I must call your attention to the fact that in many cases we are obliged to measure the temperature of the human organism, for instance, when it is in a feverish condition. This will show you the considerable importance of the relationship of the unknown being of heat to the human organism. We will deal later with the extreme conditions we encounter in chemical and technical processes. A proper attitude toward the nature of heat's relationship to the human organism cannot be attained, however, on the basis of a mechanical view of heat. This is because in doing so one neglects the fact that the various human organs are quite different in their sensitivity to heat, that the heart, liver, lungs all differ greatly in their capacity to react to the being of heat. In considering heat solely from the physical point of view, no foundation is laid for real study of certain symptoms of disease, since the organs' varying capacity to react to heat escapes attention. We are in no position today to apply to the organic world the physical views on the nature of heat built up in the course of the nineteenth century. This is obvious to anyone with an eye to see the harm done by modern physical "research," as it is called, to the higher branches of knowledge concerning themselves with the nature of the organism. Therefore, certain questions must be asked, questions that call above all for clear, lucid ideas. In the so-called "exact sciences," nothing has done more harm than the introduction of unclear, fuzzy ideas.

What does it really mean, then, when I say that I get different sensations if I put my fingers in the right and left hand vessels and then into a vessel with a liquid of an intermediate temperature? Is there really something objective in the conceptual determination of heat that is different from the so-called objective determination with the thermometer? Suppose that you now put thermometers in these two vessels instead of your fingers. You will get different readings depending on whether you observe the thermometer in one vessel or the other. If you then place the two thermometers instead of your fingers into the middle vessel, the mercury will also act differently in the two thermometers. In one it will rise, in the other it will fall. You see the thermometer does not behave differently from your sensations. In thinking about the phenomenon, there is no distinction between the two thermometers and the sensation of your fingers. In both cases, exactly the same thing occurs, namely, a difference is shown from the immediately preceding condition. And our sensation depends on the fact that within ourselves we do not have any zero or reference point. If we had such a reference point, we would establish not merely the immediate sensation but would have an apparatus to relate the temperature subjectively perceived to such a reference point. Just as we do with thermometers, we would then attach something to the phenomenon that is not really inherent in it, namely the variation from the reference point. You see, therefore, that for the construction of our concept of the process there is no difference.

It is questions such as these that must be raised today if we are to clarify our ideas regarding the theory of heat, for all the present ideas on these things are essentially unclear. Do not assume that this is of no consequence. Our whole life is bound up with this fact that we have no temperature reference point within us. If we could establish such a reference point within us, it would necessitate an entirely different state of consciousness, a different soul life. It is precisely because the reference point, the zero point, is hidden for us that we lead the kind of life we do.

Many things in life, in the human organism and in the animal organism too, depend on the fact that we do not perceive certain processes in us. Think what it would be like if you had to experience subjectively everything that goes on in your organism.

Suppose you had to be aware of all the details of your digestive process. A great deal concerning our condition of life depends on the fact that we do not bring to consciousness certain things taking place within our organism. We do not carry consciously within us a temperature reference point – we are not thermometers. To attain a comprehensive grasp of the physical, therefore, it is not sufficient to make this distinction between subjective and objective.

This has been a loose point in human thinking since the time of the ancient Greeks. It had to be so, but it cannot remain so in the future. The ancient Greek philosophers – Zeno[3], in particular – had already oriented human thinking about certain processes in a way strikingly opposed to outer reality. I must call your attention to these things even at the risk of seeming pedantic.

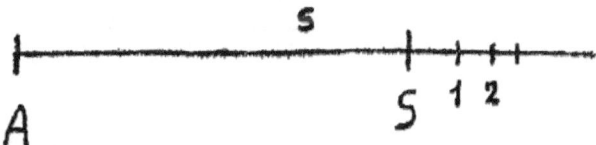

Recall the problem of Achilles and the tortoise, a problem I have often spoken about. Let us assume we have here the distance s travelled by Achilles (A); let us say it takes him a certain time. This is how fast he can run. And here we have the tortoise (S) who has a headstart (AS) on Achilles. Achilles runs after the tortoise. Let us take the moment when Achilles arrives at S. The tortoise keeps running. Achilles has to run after him. During the time he covers the distance AS the tortoise has arrived at 1. By the time Achilles has covered the distance $S1$, the tortoise has arrived at 2. Since the problem stated that Achilles has to cover every point covered by the tortoise, the tortoise will always be a little ahead and Achilles can never catch up with him.

This is generally treated by people in much the same way that quite a few of you here would treat the manner. I can tell just by looking at you. You say to yourself that you know very well that Achilles will naturally catch up with the tortoise very quickly. You think that it is simply stupid to draw the conclusion that Achilles must always cover the earlier path, that the tortoise remains ahead, and that Achilles will never catch up with him –

he whole thing is absurd, you say. But it is not right to say that, because the conclusion is absolutely compelling and binding; nothing can be said against it. It is not foolish to come to this conclusion; considering only the logic of the matter, it is remarkably clever, it is a necessary conclusion and cannot be avoided.

Now what is the basis of this dilemma? As long as you merely think, you cannot think otherwise than the premise requires. But as a matter of fact, you do not depend on thinking strictly, but instead you look at the reality and realize that it is obvious that Achilles will soon catch up with the tortoise. In doing this, you uproot thinking by means of reality and abandon the pure thought process. There is no point in admitting the premises and then saying, "Anyone who thinks this way is stupid." Through thinking alone we get nothing out of the proposition but the conclusion that Achilles will never catch up with the tortoise. And why not? Because when we apply our thinking absolutely to reality, then our conclusions are not in accord with the facts. They cannot be. When we turn our rational thinking on reality, it does not help us at all that we establish so-called truths which turn out to be untrue. For in our thinking we must conclude that if Achilles follows the tortoise he passes through each point the tortoise passes through. In the realm of ideas this is so, but in reality he does nothing of the kind. His stride is greater than that of the tortoise; he does not pass through each point of the path of the tortoise. We must therefore consider what Achilles really does and not simply limit ourselves to mere thinking. Then we arrive at different results. People do not bother about these things, but in reality they are extraordinarily important. Today especially, in our present scientific development, they are extremely important. For only if we understand that much of our thinking misses the phenomena of nature when we go from observation to so-called explanation, only in this case will we acquire the proper attitude toward these things.

The observable, however, is something that needs only to be described. I can do the following, for instance, and it calls simply for a description. Here is a ball that I will pass through this opening. I will now warm the ball slightly. Now you see it does not go through. It will go through only when it has cooled sufficiently. As soon as I cool it by pouring cold water on it, the ball goes through the opening again. This is an observation, and I need only describe it. Let us suppose, however, that I begin to theorize. I will do this in a sketchy way in order simply to introduce the matter. Here is the ball, which consists of a certain

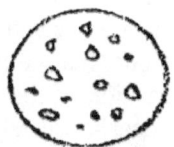

number of small parts – molecules, atoms – as you like. This is not simply observation but something added to observation in theory. At this moment I have left what has been observed, and in doing so I assume an extremely tragic role. Only those in a position to have insight into these things can realize this tragedy. For you see, if you investigate whether Achilles can catch up with the tortoise, you may indeed begin by thinking that "Achilles must pass over every point covered by the tortoise and can never catch up with it." This may be strictly demonstrated. Then you can do an experiment. You can place the tortoise ahead and Achilles, or someone else who does not run as fast as Achilles, in the rear. At every moment you can show that observation furnishes the opposite of what you conclude from reasoning. The person soon catches up with the tortoise and passes it.

When you theorize about a sphere, however, speculating about how its atoms and molecules are arranged, you abandon the possibility of observation, you cannot in such a case look into the matter and investigate it – you can only theorize. And in this realm too you will do no better than you did when you applied your thinking to the course of Achilles. That is, you carry the whole incompleteness of your logic into your thinking about something that cannot be made the object of observation. This is the tragedy. We build explanation upon explanation, at the same time abandoning observation, and we think we have explained things simply because we have erected hypotheses and theories. And the consequence of this forced reliance on our mere thinking is that this same thinking fails us the moment we are able to observe. It no longer agrees with the observation.

I already pointed out this distinction in the previous course[4] when I indicated the sharp boundary between kinematics and mechanics. Kinematics describes mere motion phenomena or equilibrium phenomena, but it is restricted to verifying the data of observation. The moment we pass over from kinematics to mechanics, where concepts of force and mass are brought in, we cannot rely on thinking alone, but we begin simply to read off what is given from observation of the phenomena. With mere thinking we are unable to deal adequately even with the simplest physical processes where mass plays a role. All nineteenth century theories are such that in order to verify them it would be necessary to do experiments with atoms and molecules. The fact that they have been shown to have a practical application in limited fields makes no difference. The principle applies to the small as well as to the large.

You may recall that in my lectures I have often called attention to certain theories that come into our considerations wearing scientific garb. I have often said that from what the physicists have theorized about heat relations and related things they get certain notions about the sun. They describe what they call the "physical conditions" on the sun and make certain claims that the facts support the description. I have often told you that if the physicists could really take a trip to the sun they would be tremendously surprised when they saw that none of their theorizing based on terrestrial conditions agreed with the realities found on the sun. These matters have a very practical value now, a value for the development of science in our time. Just recently news went forth to the world that after infinite pains the findings of certain English investigators regarding bending starlight in cosmic space had been confirmed and could now be presented to a learned group in Berlin. It was correctly stated there that the investigations of Einstein[5] and others concerning the theory of relativity had received a certain amount of confirmation. It was also stated that final confirmation could be secured only when sufficient progress had been made to make a spectral analysis of the behavior of light at the time of a solar eclipse. Then, they claimed, it would be possible to see what instruments available at present have failed to determine. This was the information given at the last meeting of the Berlin Physics Society.[6] It is remarkably interesting. Naturally the next step is to seek a way really to investigate the light of the sun by spectral analysis. The method is to be by means of instruments not available today. Then certain things that can already be discovered by spiritual science today can simply be confirmed afterwards.[7]

As you know, it is the same with many things that have come along from time to time and been clarified later by physical experiments. But people will come to realize the fact that it is simply impossible for people to apply to conditions on the sun or to cosmic space notions that have been derived from heat phenomena available to observation in the terrestrial sphere. It will be understood that the sun's corona and similar phenomena have antecedents not included in the observations made under terrestrial conditions. Just as our thinking leads us astray when we abandon observation and theorize our way through a world of atoms and molecules, so we fall into error when we go out into the macrocosm and apply to the sun what we have determined from observations under earthly conditions. Such a method has led to the belief that the sun is a kind of glowing gas ball, but the sun is by no means a glowing ball of gas.

Consider a moment – we have matter here on earth. All earthly matter has a certain degree of intensity in its action. This may be measured in one way or another, by density or the like – in any way you wish – it has a certain intensity of action. This may become zero. In other words, we may have apparently empty space. But this is not yet the end, inasmuch as there is an end. I can illustrate to you that empty space is not the ultimate condition: assume that you had a son and that you said to yourself, "He is a fool. I made over a small property to him, but he has begun to squander it. At least he can't end up with less than nothing. He may finally have nothing, but I comfort myself with the thought that he cannot go any further once he has nothing!" But you may now be disillusioned as the fellow begins to go into debt. Then he does not stop at nothing, he ends up with less than nothing. This has a very real meaning. As his parent, you end up with less if he goes into debt than if he stopped when he had nothing.

The same sort of thing applies to conditions on the sun. It is not usually considered as empty space, but it is considered in terms of the greatest possible rarefaction; it is postulated that the sun consists of rarefied, glowing gas. What we must actually do, though, in considering the sun is to go first to a condition of emptiness, to zero, and then to go beyond this. For what we would find in the sun would not be comparable at all to our conditions of matter, would not even be comparable to our empty space, which corresponds to zero; rather it goes even further than empty space. It is in a condition of negative material intensity. At the place where the sun is we would find a hole going into empty space. There is less there than empty space. Therefore all the effects to be observed on the sun must be considered as suction effects, not as pressure effects or the like. The sun's corona, for instance, must not be thought of as it is considered by the modern physicist. It must be considered in such a way that we become conscious not of forces radiating outward, as appearances would indicate, but of suction effects from the hole in space, from the negation of matter. Here our logic fails us. Here our thinking is unable to grasp the macrocosmic, as it is unable to grasp the microcosmic. In the case I have cited we can only theorize about atomic particles.

When we subjectively evaluate the heat conditions of our environment, we are not actually experiencing heat conditions; we are actually experiencing differences. The thermometer also shows differences. We experience the differences between our own heat state and that to which we relate. According to the facts, this is what the thermometer also does. By establishing a zero point, which has no intrinsic relevance to the facts at hand, we have only concealed the decisive issue. Here we have to consider an exceptionally important point. If we direct our attention to the phenomena of light, the situation is such that we observe these phenomena essentially with one organ that is quite isolated in our organism. I have spoken about this in the previous course. Therefore we actually never observe light – light is an abstraction – rather we observe color phenomena. When we subjectively observe heat, then the organ of sensation, of receptivity, is our entire organism. Our whole organism corresponds in this sensation to the eye in the case of light. There is no isolated organ; we respond with our whole body to heat conditions. The fact that we may use our finger, for instance, to perceive a heat condition does not change this fact. The finger corresponds to a portion of the eye. While the eye, therefore, is an isolated organ and functions as such to objectify the world of light as color, this is not the case for heat. We are heat organs in our entirety, as it were. Because of this, however, the outer condition that gives rise to heat does not come to us in as isolated a form as the condition that gives rise to light. Our eye is objectified within our organism. We cannot experience heat in an analogous manner to light because we are one with the heat. Imagine that you could not see colors with your eye but only different degrees of brightness, and that the colors as such remained entirely subjective, were only feelings. You would never see colors; you would speak of light and dark, but the colors would evoke in you no response, and it is thus with the perception of heat. The differences you perceive in the case of light due to the fact that your eye is an isolated organ you do not perceive at all in the case of heat. However, they live in you. Thus when you speak of blue and red, these colors are considered to be outside you. When the analogous phenomenon is met in the case of heat, that which corresponds to the blue and the red is within you. It is you yourself. Therefore you do not define it.

This requires us to adopt an entirely different method for the observation of the objective being of heat from the method we use for the observation of the objective being of light.

Nothing had so great a misleading effect on the observers of the nineteenth century as this general tendency to unify things schematically. You find everywhere in physiological theories a "physiology of the senses." As though there were such a thing! As though there were something of which it could be said in general, "The same facts hold good for the ear as for the eye, or even for the sense of touch or sense of warmth." It is an absurdity to speak of a physiology of the senses and to say that a sense perception is this or that. It is only possible to speak of the perception of the eye itself, or the perception of the ear itself, and likewise of our entire organism as a sense organ for warmth, and so on. These are very different things. Only meaningless abstractions result from a uniform consideration of the senses, but you find everywhere the tendency to make generalizations about these things. The result is to draw conclusions that would be humorous if they were not so harmful to our whole life.

If someone says, "Here is a boy that another boy has given a thrashing," and then it is also asserted that, "Yesterday he was whipped by his teacher; his teacher gave him a thrashing," then in both cases there is a thrashing given. It could be said that between these two cases "there is no difference." Am I to conclude from this that a bad boy who dealt out today's whipping and the teacher who administered yesterday's are moved by the same inner motives? That would be absurd, it would be impossible. But now the following experiment is carried out. It is known that when light rays are reflected by a concave mirror under the right conditions, the reflected rays become parallel. When these are picked up by another concave mirror distant from the first, they are concentrated and focused so that an intensified light appears at the focus. The same experiment is made with so-called heat rays. Again it can be demonstrated that these too can be focused by a concave mirror – a thermometer will show that a point of high heat intensity develops at the focal point. Here we have the same process as in the case of the light; therefore it is said that heat and light are fundamentally the same sort of thing. The thrashing of yesterday and the one of today are the same thing. If a person came to such a conclusion in practical life, he would be considered a fool. In science, however, as it is pursued today, he is no fool but a highly respected individual.

It is because of things like this that we should strive for clear and lucid concepts, without which we will not progress. Without them physics cannot contribute to a universal worldview. In the realm of physics especially, it is necessary to press forward to clear and vivid concepts.

You know quite well from what was made clear to you in my last course, at least to a certain extent, that Goethe brought some degree of order into the physics of light phenomena, but no recognition has been given to him. In the realm of heat phenomena it is now exceptionally difficult, because in the post-Goethean era the whole study of heat has been plunged into a chaos of theoretical considerations. In the nineteenth century, the mechanical theory of heat, as it is called, has resulted in error upon error. It has applied concepts verifiable only by observation to a realm not accessible to observation. Anyone who believes himself able to think, but who in reality may not be able to do so, can easily propose theories. The following is such a theory: a gas enclosed on all sides by a vessel consists of gas particles, but

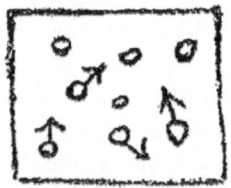

these particles are not at rest; they are in a state of continuous motion. Since these particles are in continuous motion and are small and conceived of as separated by relatively great distances, they do not collide with each other often but only occasionally. When they do so, they rebound. Their motion is changed by this mutual bombardment. Now when one sums up all the various slight impacts there comes about a pressure on the wall of the vessel. One can also measure how great the temperature is. It is then said that the particles in the vessel are in a certain state of motion, bombarding each other. The whole mass is in rapid motion, the particles bombarding each other and striking the wall. If the vessel is heated, the particles may move faster and faster, striking the wall harder. Then it may be asked, "What is heat?" and the conclusion is that it is motion of these small particles. To be sure, these ideas have suffered somewhat under the influence of the facts, but only superficially.[8] The entire method of thinking still rests on the same foundation. A great deal of pride is taken in this so-called mechanical theory of heat, for it seems to explain so many things.

It supposedly explains, for instance, how pressure or work is transformed into heat when I rub my finger over a surface. I can then turn heat back into work, in the steam engine for instance, where I secure motion by means of heat. A very comfortable working concept has been built up along these lines. It is said that when we observe these things objectively going on in space, they are mechanical processes. The locomotive and the cars all move forward, etc., when, now, through some sort of work I produce here, what has really happened is that the outer observable motion has been transformed into motion of the smallest particles. This is a comfortable theory. It can be said that everything in the world is dependent on motion and that observable motion is merely transformed into motion that is not observable. The latter we perceive as heat, heat in reality being nothing but the impact and collision of the little gas particles striking each other and the walls of the vessel. This is the Clausius[9] theory of what goes on in a gas-filled space.

This is the theory that has resulted from applying the method of the Achilles proposition to something not accessible to observation. It is not noticed that the same impossible grounds are used as when such thinking is applied to Achilles and the tortoise. Within a gas-filled space things are very different from the way we imagine them to be when we carry over the observable into unobservable concepts.

My purpose today is to present this idea to you in an introductory way. From this consideration you can see that the fundamental method of thinking that originated during the nineteenth century begins to fail, for a large part of the method rests on the principle of calculating from observed facts by means of the differential concept. When the observed conditions in a gas-filled space at a certain pressure are set down as differentials in accordance with the idea that we are dealing with the movements of ultimate particles, then the belief follows that, by integrating, something real is arrived at. What must be understood is this: when we go from ordinary methods of calculation to differential equations, it is not possible to integrate with these differential equations without losing all contact with reality. This false notion of the relation of the integral to the differential has led the physics of the nineteenth century into false ideas of reality. It must be made clear that in certain instances one can set up differentials, but what is obtained as a differential cannot be thought of as being able to be integrated without leading us into the realm of the ideal as opposed to the real. Understanding this is very important in our relation to nature.

You see, when I initiate a certain process of transformation, I say that work is performed, heat produced, and from this heat work can again be secured by a reversal of the process. I will show you later the extent to which this applies to the inorganic in regard to heat phenomena. But an organic process cannot be reversed so simply. There are also great inorganic processes that are not reversible, such as the planetary processes. We cannot imagine a reversal of the process that goes on in the plant from the formation of the roots, through the flower and fruit formation. The process takes its course from the seed to the setting of the fruit. It cannot be reversed like an inorganic process. This fact does not enter into our calculation. Even when we remain in the inorganic, there are certain macrocosmic processes for which our calculation is not valid. Suppose you were able to set down a formula for the growth of a plant: it would be very complicated, but assume that you have such a formula. Certain terms in it could never be made negative, because to do so would be to disagree with reality. I could not represent the formation of the blossom out of the formation of the leaf with negative values. I would not be able to reverse the process. I am also unable to reverse reality in the face of the vaster phenomena of the world. This does not apply, however, to calculating. If I have an eclipse of the moon today, I can easily calculate how in times past, in the period of Thales, for instance, there was an eclipse of the moon. That is, I can reverse the process only in calculation, but in reality the process is not reversible. We cannot pass from the present state of the earth to former states, to an eclipse of the moon at the time of Thales, for instance, simply by reversing the process in calculation. A calculation may be made forward or backward, but usually reality does not agree with the calculation. The calculation passes over reality.

We must become aware of the extent to which our concepts and calculations are only conceptual in their content. In spite of the fact that our calculations are reversible, in reality these processes are not reversible. This is essential, since we will see that the whole theory of heat is built on questions of the following sort: to what extent are heat processes within nature reversible and to what extent are they irreversible?

Lecture II

Stuttgart,
March 2, 1920

Yesterday I touched upon the fact that bodies expand under the influence of heat. Today we will first consider how solid bodies expand when acted upon by the being of warmth. In order that these things make a real impression on us so that we can use them properly in our teaching – and at this stage the matter is quite simple and elementary: we have set up this apparatus with an iron bar. We will heat the iron bar and make its expansion visible by noting the movements of this lever arm over a scale. When I press here (P) with my finger, the pointer moves upward (see drawing).

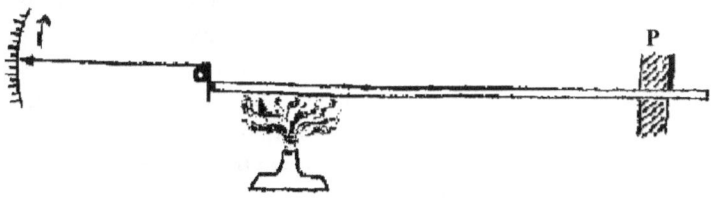

You can see when we heat the rod that the pointer does move upward, which indicates for you the fact that the rod expands. The pointer moves upward at once. You will also notice that with continued heating the pointer moves more and more, showing that the expansion increases with the temperature. If I had a rod consisting of a different metal from the rod here, and if we measured precisely the amount of its expansion, it would be found to be different from what it is here. We would find that different substances expanded varying amounts. We would thus be able to establish at once that the expansion, the degree of the rod's elongation, depended on the substance. At this point we will leave out of account the fact that we are dealing with a cylinder, and we will assume that we have a body of a certain length without breadth or thickness; we will therefore consider the expansion in one direction only. To make the matter clear we may consider it as follows: here is a rod, considered simply as a length, and we denote the length by l_0, the length of the rod at the original temperature, the starting temperature. The length attained by the rod when it is heated to a temperature t we will indicate by l.

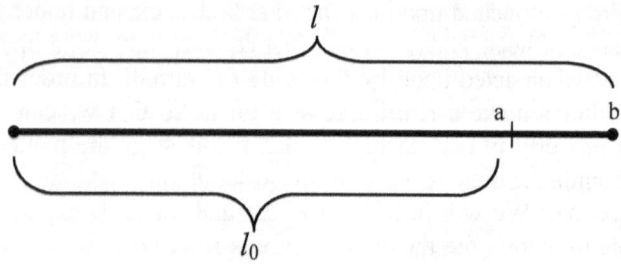

Now I said that the rod expanded varying amounts depending upon the substance of which it is composed. We can express the amount of expansion, as shown in the figure from *a* to *b*, by a fraction giving the relation of the expansion to the original length of the rod. Let us denote this relative expansion by α. Then we know the length of the rod after expansion, for the length l after expansion may be considered as made up of the original length l_0 and the small addition to this length contributed by the expansion. This must be added on. Since I have denoted by α the fraction giving the ratio of the expansion to the original length, I get the expansion for a given substance by multiplying l_0 by α.[10] Since the expansion is greater the higher the temperature, I also have to multiply by the temperature t. Thus I can say the length of the rod after expansion is

$$l = l_0 + l_0\, \alpha t = l_0\, (1 + \alpha t)$$

Stated in words this means that if I wish to determine the length of a rod expanded by heat, I must multiply the original length by a factor consisting of *1* plus the temperature times the relative expansion of the substance under consideration. Physicists have become accustomed to calling α the expansion coefficient of the substance considered.

Here I have considered a rod. Rods without breadth and thickness do not exist in reality. In reality bodies have three dimensions. If we proceed from the longitudinal expansion to the expansion of an assumed surface, the formula may be changed as follows: let us assume now that we are to observe the expansion of a surface instead of simply an expansion in one dimension. Here is a surface. This surface extends in two directions,

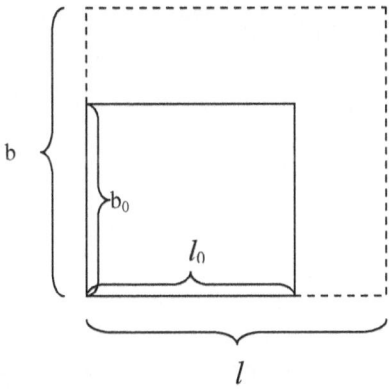

and, after warming, both will have increased in extent. We must therefore consider not only the longitudinal expansion to 1 but also an increase in the breadth to b. Taking first the original length l_0, we have as before the expansion in this direction to l or

$$l = l_0(1 + \alpha t) \tag{1}$$

Considering now the breadth b_0, which expands to b, I must write the formula as follows:

$$b = b_0(1 + \alpha t) \tag{2}$$

(It is obvious that the same rule will apply here as in the case of the length.) Now, you know that the area of the surface is obtained by multiplying the length by the breadth. The original area I get by multiplying b_0 by l_0, and after expansion by multiplying $l_0 (1 + \alpha t)$ and $b_0 (1 + \alpha t)$.

$$lb = l_0(1 + \alpha t)\, b_0 (1 + \alpha t) \qquad (3)$$

I thus arrive at:

$$lb = l_0\, b_0\, (1 + \alpha t)^2 \qquad (4)$$

which can be expressed as:

$$lb = l_0\, b_0(1 + 2\alpha t + \alpha^2 t^2) \qquad (5)$$

This gives the formula for the expansion of the surface. If you now imagine thickness (d) added to the surface, this thickness must be treated in the same way, and then I can write:

$$l\,b\,d = t_0\, b_0\, d_0\, (1 + 3\alpha t + 3\alpha^2 t^2 + \alpha^3 t^3) \qquad (6)$$

When you look at this formula I will ask you please to note the following: in the first two terms of (6) you see t raised no higher than the first power; in the third term you see the second power, and in the fourth term it is raised to the third power. Note especially these last two terms of the formula for expansion. Observe that when we deal with the expansion of a three-dimensional body, we obtain a formula containing the third power of the temperature. It is extremely important to keep in mind this fact that here we encounter the third power of the temperature.

Now I must always remember that we are here in the Waldorf School, and I must present everything in its relation to how we might teach it. I will therefore call your attention to the fact that the same introduction I have made here is presented very differently in the ordinary physics textbooks. I will now tell you how it is presented in the average physics textbook. It would be said that α is a ratio. It is a fraction. The expansion is relatively very small compared to the original length of the rod. When I have a fraction whose denominator is greater than its numerator, if I then square it or cube it, I get a much smaller fraction. For if I square a third, I get a ninth, and when I cube a third I get a twenty-seventh. That is, the third power is a very, very small fraction. α is a fraction whose denominator is usually very large.[10] Therefore most physics books say: if I square α to get α^2 or cube it to get α^3, with which I multiply t^3, these are very small fractions and can simply be dropped out. The average physics text says that we simply drop these last terms of the expansion formula and write $l \times b \times d$ – this is the volume and I will write it as V. The volume of an expanded body heated to a certain temperature is thus expressed as:

$$V = V_0 (1 + 3\alpha t) \qquad (7)$$

The expansion of a solid body is expressed by this formula. It is considered that since the fraction a squared and cubed gives such small quantities, these can be dropped out. You recognize this as the treatment in the physics texts. In doing this, however, the most important thing for a really appropriate theory of heat is stricken out. This will become clear as we progress further.

Expansion under the influence of heat is shown not only by solids but by fluids as well. Here we have a fluid colored so that you can see it. We will warm this colored fluid (see drawing). You will now see that after some time the colored fluid column will rise, and from this you will conclude that liquids expand as do solid bodies. You see the colored fluid rise. The fluid expands through warming.

We can investigate the expansion of a gaseous body in a similar way. For this purpose we have air here in this vessel which simply enters from outside (see drawing). Now we shut the air into the vessel and warm it. Notice that here is a tube communicating with the vessel and containing a liquid whose level is the same in both arms of the tube. When we warm the air

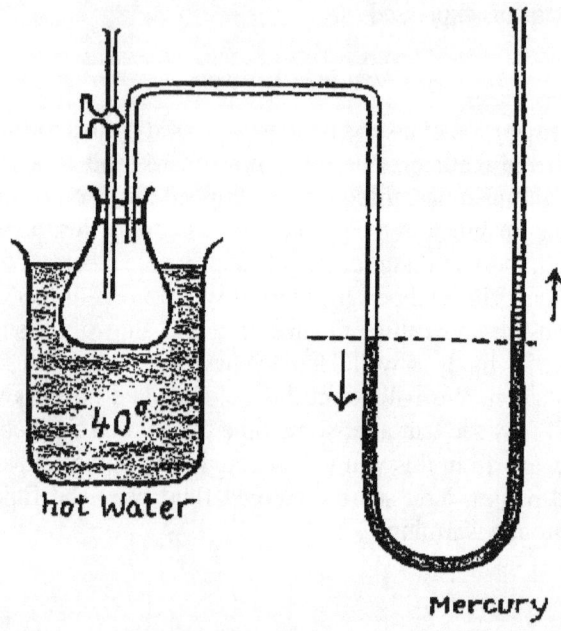

in the vessel, the air constituting a gaseous body, you will see what happens. We will warm it by immersing the vessel in water heated to a temperature of 40° C. You see, the mercury at once rises on the right. Why does it rise? Because the gaseous body in the vessel expands. The air streams into the tube, presses on the mercury (left), and the pressure forces the mercury column on the right up into the tube. From this you see that the gaseous body has expanded. We may therefore conclude that solid, liquid, and gaseous bodies all expand under the influence of the being of heat, as yet unknown to us.

We must take into account something very important now as we proceed from the study of the expansion of solids through the expansion of liquids to the expansion of a gas. I have already stated that α, the relation of the expansion to the original length of the rod, differed for different substances. If, by means of further experiments that cannot be performed here, we were to investigate α for various fluids, we would again find different values for various fluid substances. When we investigate α for gaseous bodies,[11] however, a peculiar thing reveals itself, namely that a is not different for various gases but that this expansion coefficient, as it is called, remains the same and has a constant value of about $1/273$. This fact is of tremendous importance, showing us that as we advance from solid bodies to gases, genuinely new relations arise under the influence of heat. It appears that different gases are related to heat simply according to their property of being gases and not according to variations in the nature of the matter composing them. The condition of being a gas is, so to speak, a property that may be shared in common by all gaseous bodies. We see, indeed, that for all gases known to us on earth, the property of being a gas gathers together into a unity this property of expanding. Keep in mind now that the facts of expansion under the influence of heat oblige us to say that when we proceed from solid bodies to gases, the different expansion values found in the case of solids are transformed into a kind of unity or single coefficient of expansion for gases. The solid condition in our earthly domain is bound up with a differentiation of substantiality. Thus, if I may express myself cautiously, the solid condition may be said to be associated with an individualization of the material condition. Modern physics pays scant attention to this circumstance. No attention is paid to it, because the most important things are obscured by the fact of striking out certain values in the calculation that cannot be handled adequately.

To gain a deeper insight into these matters we must call on the history of the development of physics. All the ideas current in modern physics textbooks and ruling the methods by which the facts of physics are handled are really not so old. They began for the most part in the seventeenth century and took their fundamental character from the new impulse given by a certain scientific spirit in Europe through the *Accademia del Cimento* in Florence. This was founded in 1657, and many experiments in quite different fields were carried out there, especially, however, experiments dealing with heat, acoustics, and tone. We can realize how recent our ordinary ideas are when we look into some of the special apparatus of the *Accademia del Cimento*. It was there, for instance, that the groundwork for our modern thermometry was laid. At this academy they observed for the first time how mercury behaves in a glass tube ending at the bottom in a closed cylinder when the mercury filling the tube is heated. In the *Accademia del Cimento* it was first noticed that there is an apparent contradiction between the experiments where the expansion of liquids may be observed and another type of experiment.

The generalization had been attained that liquids expand. But when the experiment was carried out with mercury, it was noticed that it first fell when the tube was heated and only after that began to rise. This was first explained in the seventeenth century, and quite simply, by saying: "When heat is applied, the outer glass is heated at the start and expands. The space occupied by the mercury becomes greater. It sinks at first and begins to rise only when the heat has penetrated into the mercury itself." Ideas of this sort have been current since the seventeenth century. At the same time, however, people were backward in grasping the real ideas necessary to understand physics, since until this period, the Renaissance, Europe was little inclined to trouble itself with scientific concepts of this kind. It was the time set aside for the spread of Christianity. This in a certain sense hindered the process of arriving at concepts concerning physical phenomena. Then during the Renaissance, when people became acquainted with the ideas of ancient Greece, the situation was somewhat as follows. On the one hand, encouraged by all sorts of support, institutions arose where it was possible to do experiments, like the *Accademia del Cimento*. The course of physical phenomena could be observed directly. On the other hand, people had become unaccustomed to constructing concepts about things. They had lost the habit of really following things in thought. The ancient Greek ideas were now taken up again, but they were no longer understood. Thus the concept of fire or heat, or as much of this as could be understood, was assumed to be the same as was held in ancient Greece. That great chasm between thought and what can be derived from the observation of experiments was established at this time. This chasm has widened more and more since the seventeenth century. The art of experiment reached its full flower in the nineteenth century, but a development of clear, definite concepts did not parallel this flowering of the experimental art. And today, lacking clear, definite concepts, we often stand perplexed before phenomena revealed in the course of time by unthinking experimentation. When the way has been found not only to experiment and to observe the outer results of the experiments but really to enter into the inner nature of the phenomena, then only can these results be made fruitful for human spiritual development.

When we penetrate into the inner course of natural phenomena, it becomes very important that entirely different expansion relations arise when we proceed from solids to gases. But until the whole body of our physical concepts is extended, we will not really be able to evaluate things such as those we have been able to derive purely from the facts themselves.

Now, to the facts already determined, another one of extraordinary importance must be added. You know that a general rule can be stated, namely that if bodies are heated they expand. If they are cooled again they contract. A general law may thus be stated succinctly: "Through heating, bodies expand, through cooling they contract." You will recall, however, from your elementary physics that there are exceptions to this rule, and one exception that is of cardinal importance is the one regarding water. When water is made to expand and contract, we come upon a remarkable fact. If we have water at $8°$ C, and we cool it, it contracts at first. That goes without saying. But when the water is cooled further it does not contract but expands again. Thus the ice that is formed from water – and we will speak further of this – floats on the surface of the water since it has expanded and become less dense than the water. This is a striking phenomenon, that ice can float on the surface of water! This originates in the fact that the general law of expansion and contraction does not apply as such to water. If this were not so, if we did not have this exception, the whole arrangement of nature would be strikingly affected. If you observe a basin filled with water, or a pond, you will see that even in very cold winter weather, there is a coating of ice on the surface only and that this protects the underlying water from freezing. There is always an ice coating and underneath protected water. The irregularity that appears here is, to use a domestic expression, tremendously important in the household of nature. Now the way in which we arrive at a physical view of this that can be depended on must be in strict accordance with the principles laid down in the last course. We must avoid the path that leads to an Achilles-and-the-tortoise conclusion. We must not forget the manifested facts and must experiment with the facts in mind, that is, we must remain in the field where the accessible facts are such as to enable us to determine something. Therefore, let us hold strictly to what is observable and from this seek an explanation for the phenomena. We will stick closely to things that are readily observable, such as expansion and the irregularity in expansion that we found in water (noting that it is associated with a fluid). Such factual matters should be kept in mind, and we must remain in the world of facts. This is real Goetheanism in the realm of the physical.

Let us now consider something that is not a theory but a demonstrable fact of the outer world: when matter passes into the gaseous condition, there arises a unification of properties for all substances on the earth, and with the passage to the solid condition downward there takes place an individualizing, a differentiation.

Now if we ask ourselves how it can come about that with the passage from the solid to the gaseous through the liquid state a unification takes place, we have a great deal of difficulty answering on the basis of our available concepts. We must first ask certain fundamental questions if we are to remain in the realm of the observable. We must first ask: Whence comes the possibility generally for expansion in bodies, followed gradually by change into the gaseous state with its accompanying unification of properties?

You need only look in a general way at everything we know about the physical processes on the earth in order to come to the following conclusion: unless the action of the sun were present, we could not have all these phenomena taking place on earth through the influence of the being of heat. You must pay close attention to the enormous significance that the being of the sun has for earthly phenomena. And when you consider this, which is simply a matter of fact, you are obliged to say that this unification of properties that takes place in the passage from the solid through the fluid and into the gaseous state could not happen if the earth were left to itself. Only when we go beyond mere earthly relationships can we find a firm standpoint for our consideration of these things. In admitting this, however, we have made a very far-reaching admission. For by putting the *Accademia del Cimento*'s way of thinking, and all that went with it, in place of the above-mentioned point of view, the ancient concepts still useful in Greece were robbed of all their extraterrestrial characteristics. And you will soon see that, purely from the facts, without any historical help, we are going to come back to these extraterrestrial characteristics. It will perhaps be easier to gain your understanding if I make a short historical sketch now.

I have already said that the real meaning of the ideas and concepts of physical phenomena still prevalent in ancient Greece has been lost. Experimentation was begun, ideas and concepts were taken up parrot-fashion, without the inner thought process that had accompanied them in ancient Greece.

Everything that the Greeks had included in these physical concepts was forgotten. The Greeks had not simply said, "solid, liquid, gaseous"; what they expressed may be translated into our own language as follows:

> Whatever was *solid* was called *earth* in ancient Greece;
> Whatever was *fluid* was called *water* in ancient Greece;
> Whatever was *gaseous* was called *air* in ancient Greece.

It is totally wrong to think that we can carry our own meaning of the words *earth*, *water*, and *air* over into ancient writings in which Greek influence was dominant and assume that the corresponding words have the same meaning there. When we come across the word *water* in ancient writings, we must translate it with our word *fluidity*, and the word *earth* with our word *solids*. Only in this way can we correctly translate the ancient writings. But a profound significance is implicit in this. The use of the word *earth* to indicate solids implied especially that this solid condition falls under the laws prevailing on the planet earth (as stated above, we will arrive at these things in the following lectures from the facts themselves – they are presented today in this historical sketch simply to further your understanding of the matter). Solids were designated as *earth* because it was desired to convey this idea: when a body is solid it is under the influence of earthly laws in every respect. On the other hand, when a body was spoken of as *water*, then it was not merely under earthly laws but influenced by the entire planetary system. The forces active in fluid bodies, in *water*, spring not merely from the earth but from the planetary system. The forces of Mercury, Mars, and so on are active in everything that is fluid. But they act in such a way that they are oriented according to the position of the planets, which shows a kind of resultant in the fluidity.

The feeling therefore was that only solid bodies, designated as *earth*, were solely under the earthly system of laws, and that when a body melted it was influenced from outside the earth. And when a gaseous body was called *air*, the feeling was that such a body was under the unifying influence of the sun. (These things are presented simply in a historical way at this point.) This body was lifted out of the earthly and the merely planetary and stood under the unifying influence of the sun. Earthly air beings were looked upon in this way: the forces of the sun were essentially active in their configuration, their inner arrangement and substance. Ancient physics had a cosmic character. It was willing to take into account the forces actually present in fact. For the Moon, Mercury, Mars, etc. are facts. But people lost the sources of this view of things and were at first unable to develop a need for new sources. They therefore could only conceive that since solid bodies in their expansion and in their whole configuration fell under the laws of the earth, liquid and gaseous bodies must do likewise. You might say that it would never occur to a physicist to deny that the sun warmed the air, etc. Indeed, he does not do this, but since he proceeds from concepts such as I characterized yesterday, which delineate the action of the sun according to ideas springing from observations on the earth, he explains the sun in terrestrial terms instead of explaining the terrestrial in solar terms.

The essential thing is that the consciousness of certain things was completely lost in the period extending from the fifteenth to the seventeenth centuries. The consciousness that our earth is a member of the whole solar system, and that consequently every single thing on the earth has to do with the whole solar system, was lost. The feeling was also lost that the solidity of bodies originated through the earthly element emancipating itself from the cosmic, tearing itself free to attain independent laws, while the lawfulness of the gaseous realm, for example, the air, remained under the unifying influence of the sun as it affected the earth as a whole. This is what has led to the necessity of explaining things terrestrially, things that formerly received a cosmic explanation. Since man no longer looked to the activity of planetary forces when a solid body changed to a fluid, as when ice becomes fluid – changes to water – since the forces were no longer sought in the planetary system, they had to be placed within the fluid body itself. It was necessary to rationalize and theorize over the way in which the atoms and molecules were arranged in such a body. And the ability from within to bring about the change from solid to liquid, from liquid to gas, had to be ascribed to these unfortunate molecules and atoms. Formerly such a change was considered to act through what was actually given in space from the cosmic regions beyond the earth.

In this way we must understand the transition of the concepts of physics as shown especially in the crass materialism of the *Accademia del Cimento*, which flowered in the ten-year period between 1657 and 1667. You must picture to yourselves that this crass materialism arose through the gradual loss of ideas embodying the connection between the earthly and the cosmos beyond the earth. Today the necessity again faces us to realize this connection. It will not be possible to emerge from materialism unless we cease being pedantic in this field of physics. The narrow-mindedness arises simply because we go from concrete to abstract concepts, for no one loves abstract concepts more than the Philistine. He wishes to explain everything with a few formulae, a few abstract ideas. But physics cannot hope to advance if it continues to spin theories as has been the fashion ever since the materialism of the *Accademia del Cimento*. We will progress in our understanding of a field such as heat only if we seek to establish once again the connection between the terrestrial and the cosmic through wider and more comprehensive ideas than modern materialistic physics can furnish us.

Lecture III

*Stuttgart,
March 3, 1920*

Today in order to press toward the goal of our first lecture, we will consider some of the relations between the being of heat and the so-called states of aggregation. By state of aggregation I am referring to what was called earth, water, and air in the ancient view of the physical world, as I described yesterday. You are acquainted with the fact that earth, water, and air – or, as they are called today, solid, fluid, and gaseous bodies – may be transformed into one another. In this process, however, a peculiar phenomenon reveals itself in so far as heat relations are concerned.

I will first describe the phenomenon, and then we will demonstrate it in a simple fashion. If we select any solid body and heat it, it will become warmer and warmer and finally come to a point at which it will pass over from the solid to the fluid condition. By means of a thermometer we can determine that as the body gets warmer and warmer its temperature rises. At the moment when the body begins to melt, to become fluid, the thermometer ceases rising. It remains stationary until the entire body has become fluid and only begins to rise again when all of the solid is melted. Thus we can say that during the process of melting the thermometer shows no increase in temperature. It must not be concluded from this, however, that no heat is being absorbed. For if we discontinue heating, the process of melting will stop. (I will speak more of this subsequently.) Heat must be added in order to bring about melting, but the heat does not show itself in the form of an increase in temperature on the thermometer. The instrument begins to show an increase in temperature only when the melting has entirely finished and the liquid formed from the solid begins to take up the heat. Let us consider this phenomenon carefully, for it shows that in the process of the rise in temperature a discontinuity exists. We will collect a number of such facts, and these can lead us then to a view of heat without going over to some concocted theory.

We have prepared here a solid, sodium thiosulphate, which we will melt. You see here a temperature of about 25°C. Now we will proceed to heat this body, and I will ask someone to come up and watch the temperature to verify the fact that while the solid is melting the temperature actually does not rise. (Note: the thermometer went to 48°C., which is the melting point of sodium thiosulphate, and remained there until the substance had melted.) Now the thermometer rises rapidly, since the melting is complete, although it remained stationary during the entire process of melting.

Suppose we sketch this occurrence in a simple way, as follows:[12] we will visualize the temperature rise as a line sloping upward like this (see drawing). Assume we have raised the temperature to the melting point, as it is called. So far as the ther-

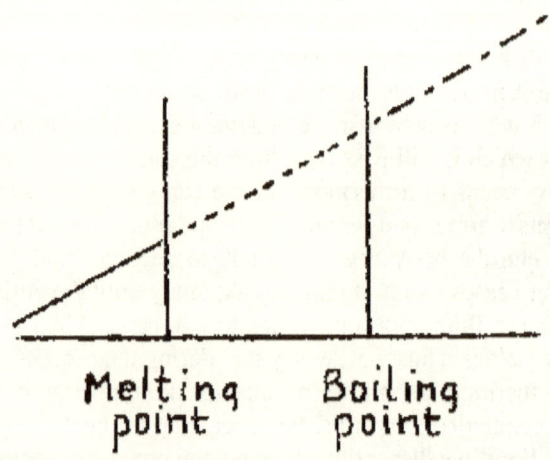

mometer shows, the temperature then becomes stationary. When heat is applied further the temperature again rises. It can be shown that through this further rise in temperature, with its corresponding addition of heat, the liquid in question expands. Now if we heat such a melted body further, the temperature rises again from the point at which melting took place (dotted line). It rises as long as the body remains fluid. We then come upon a second point at which the liquid begins to boil, to evaporate. Again we have the same phenomenon as before. The thermometer shows no further temperature rise until all the liquid has evaporated. At the moment when the fluid has evaporated, we would find that if we held a thermometer in the vapor it would again show a temperature rise (dot-dash line). You can see here that during the process of evaporation the thermometer does not indicate a rise in temperature. Here I find a second place where the thermometer remains stationary.

I will now ask you to add to the facts I have brought before you another that you will know well from ordinary experience. If you consider solids, which are our starting point, you know that they hold their shape by themselves; whatever form is given them they maintain. If I place a solid here before you, it remains as it is (see drawing, 1). If you take a fluid, that is, a body that has been made to go through the melting point by the

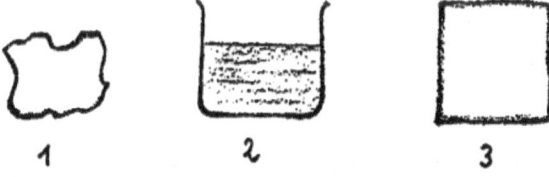

application of heat, you know that I cannot handle it piece by piece; it is necessary to place it in a vessel, and it takes the form of the vessel, forming a horizontal upper surface (2). If I take a gas – a body that has been vaporized by passing through the boiling point – I cannot keep it in an open vessel such as I use for the liquid; it will be lost. Such a gas or vapor I can hold only in a vessel closed in on all sides; otherwise the gas spreads out in all directions (3). This is the case at least for superficial observation, and we will consider the matter first in this way.

Now I would ask you to undergo the following consideration of these things with me. We do this in order to bring facts together so that we can reach a general conception of the nature of heat. How have we determined the rise in temperature? We have determined it by means of the expansion of mercury. This expansion has taken place in space. And since at our ordinary temperature mercury is a liquid, we must keep clear in our minds that it is confined in a vessel, and the three-dimensional expansion is summed up so that we get an expansion in one direction. By reducing the expansion of mercury in three dimensions to a single dimension, we have made this expansion measure the temperature rise.

Let us proceed from the starting point of this fundamental observation and consider the following: take a line (see drawing) – naturally a line can only exist in thought – and suppose that on

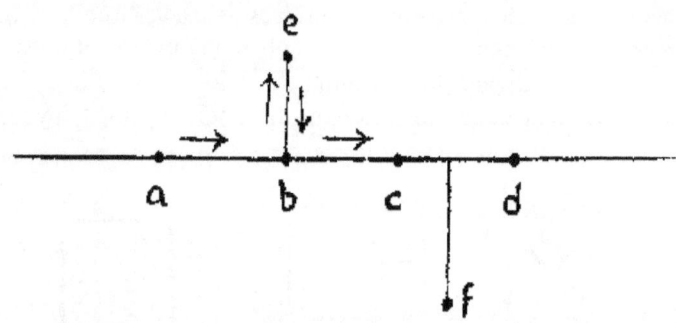

this line there lie a number of points, *a*, *b*, *c*, *d*, etc. If you wish to reach these points you can remain along the line. If, for instance, you are at this point (*a*), you can reach *c* by passing along the line. You can pass back again, and again reach the point *a*. In brief, if I wish to reach the points *a*, *b*, *c*, *d*, I can do so and remain entirely along the line. The matter is different when we consider the point *e* or the point *f*. You cannot remain on the line if you wish to reach points *e* or *f*. You must go off the line to reach these points. You have to move along the line and then off of it to get to these points.

Now assume you have a surface, let us say the surface of the blackboard, and again I locate on the surface of this board a number of points, *a*, *b*, *c* (see drawing, next page). In order to reach these points you may always remain on the surface of the blackboard. If you are at this point (*x*), you may trace your way to each of these points over a path that does not leave the blackboard. If you wish to remain on the surface of the board, however, you cannot reach this point that is at a distance in front of the board. To reach this point you must leave the surface. This consideration leads to a view of the dimensionality of space from which one can say: to reach points in one dimension,

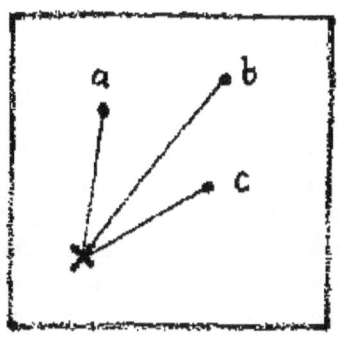

movement in this single direction suffices; to reach points outside a single dimension, however, it is not possible without leaving this dimension, and likewise one cannot pass through points in three dimensions by moving about in a single plane. What is involved when I consider the points e and f in relation to the single dimension represented by points a, b, c, d?

Imagine a being who was able to observe only one dimension and so had no conception of a second or a third dimension. Such a being would move in his one dimension just as you do in three-dimensional space. If such a being carried the point a to the position b, and the point then slipped off to e, at that moment the content of the point would simply vanish from the single dimension of this being. It would no longer exist for this being from the moment it left the single dimension of which he is aware. Likewise points outside a surface would not exist for a being aware of only two dimensions. When a point dropped out of the plane, such a being would have no way of following it – the point would disappear from the realm of his space. What kind of geometry would a one-dimensional being have? He would have a one-dimensional geometry. He would be able to speak only of distance and the like, of the laws relating to such things as they applied in a single dimension. A two-dimensional being would be able to speak of the laws of plane figures and would have a two-dimensional geometry. We human beings have to begin with a three-dimensional geometry. A being with a one-dimensional geometry would have no possibility of understanding what a point does when it leaves the single dimension. A being with a two-dimensional geometry would be unable to follow the motion of a point that left a surface and moved out in front of it, as we supposed was the case when the point left the surface of the blackboard. We human beings have a three-dimensional geometry.

Now I can also do what I am obliged to do when I reduce the three-dimensional expansion of mercury to a single dimension, as we do with a thermometer. I may draw two lines in two directions so as to form a system of axes, thus giving a coordinate system with an axis of abscissa and an axis of ordinates(see drawing). At right angles to the plane of these two, suppose we

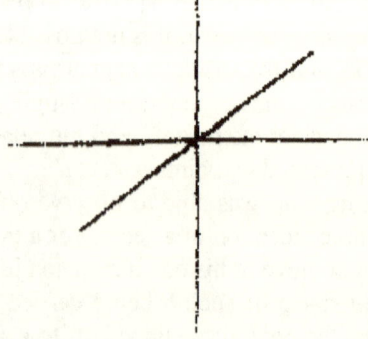

have a third axis that we will call a space line. As soon as I come either to the melting point or to the boiling point I am not in a position to proceed with this line (see drawing).

Theoretically or hypothetically there is a possibility of continuing the line. Let us assume that we can say that the rise of temperature is represented by this line (see drawing, next page). We can proceed along it and still have a point of connection with our ordinary world. But we do not, as a matter of fact, have such a point of connection. For when I draw this temperature curve and come to the melting or boiling points, I can only continue the curve from the same point (x,x in drawing) I had reached when the body had begun to melt or evaporate. You can see from this that, regarding the melting or boiling points, I am in the same position as that of the one-dimensional being when a point moves out of his first dimension into the second dimension, or of the two-dimensional being when a point disappears for him into the third dimension. When the point comes back

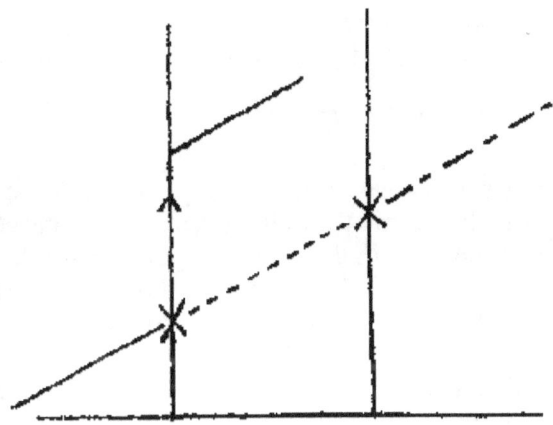

again and starts from the same place or, as in the drawing on page 34, when the point moves out to one side and returns, then it is necessary to continue the line in its one dimension. Considered simply as an observed phenomenon, when the temperature rise disappears at the melting and boiling points, it is as though my temperature curve was interrupted and I had to proceed after a time from the same point. But what is happening to the heat during this interruption falls outside the realm in which I draw my curve. I may say that I can draw this as a space curve. There is at first – note, I say *at first* – an analogy between the disappearance of the point a from the first into the second dimension and what happens to the temperature as shown by the thermometer when the mercury stands still at the melting point and the boiling point.

Now we have to establish the connection of this to another phenomenon. Please note that in linking together phenomena like this we make progress, not in elaborating some kind of theories but in bringing together phenomena so that they mutually illuminate and explain each other. This is the distinction between the physics of Goethe, which simply places phenomena side by side so that they throw light on each other, and modern physics, which tends to pass into theories and to add thought-out elaborations to the facts, for atoms and molecules are nothing but fancies added to the facts.

Let us now consider another phenomenon along with this disappearance of the temperature recorded by the thermometer during the process of melting. This other phenomenon meets us when we look at yesterday's formula. This formula was written:

$$V = V_0 (1 + 3\alpha t + 3\alpha^2 t^2 + \alpha^3 t^3)$$

You remember that I said yesterday you should pay special attention to the last two terms. It is especially important for us at this time to consider t^3, the third power of the temperature. Imagine for a moment ordinary space. In this ordinary space you speak in mathematical terms of length, breadth, and height. These are the three dimensions of space. Now when we heat a rod, as we did yesterday, we can observe the expansion of this rod. We can also note the temperature of this rod, but there is one thing we cannot prevent. We cannot prevent the rod, while it is expanding, from giving off heat to its surroundings, from streaming out or radiating heat. This we cannot prevent. It is impossible for us to *think* – note the word – of an expansion of heat in one dimension. We can indeed think of an expansion in space in one dimension, as one does in geometry in the case of a line, but we cannot under any circumstances imagine a heat expansion merely along a line. When we consider this matter, we cannot say that the propagation of heat – thought of as a curve, not in space – is fully represented pictorially with the curve I drew here (see drawing, page 37). I cannot encompass the whole process involved in heat with this curve. Something else is active besides what I can encompass with this curve. And the activity of this something changes the entire nature and being of what is shown by this curve, which I am using as a symbol for the state of heat and which may be considered equally well either arithmetically or geometrically.

We thus have a peculiar situation. When we try to grasp the heat condition – in so far as the temperature shows this condition – by means of an ordinary geometrical line, we find it cannot be done. Now this has another effect. Imagine for a moment that I have a line (see drawing). This line has a certain length, l. I square this line, and then I can represent this l^2 by a square surface. Assume that I obtain l^3 — then I can represent the third power by a cube, a solid body (see drawing). But suppose I ob-

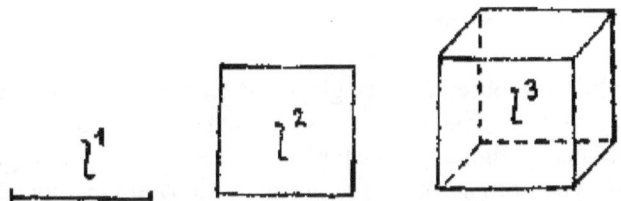

tain the fourth power, l^4 — how can I represent that? I can pass from the line to the surface, from the surface to the solid, but what can I do by following this same method if I wish to represent the fourth power? I cannot do anything if I remain in our three-dimensional space. The mathematical consideration of space shows this. But we have seen that the heat condition, in so far as it is revealed by temperature, is not expressible in spatial terms. There is something else in it. If there were not, we could conceive of the heat condition passing along a rod as confined entirely to the rod. This, however, is impossible. The consequence of this is that when I really wish to work in this realm, I ought not to look upon the powers of t in the same way as the powers of a quantity measured in space. I cannot think about the powers of t in the same way as those of l or of any other mere spatial quantity. If, for instance — and I will consider this merely hypothetically today — if I have the first power of t and find it not expressible as a line, then the second power t^2 cannot be expressed as a surface, and certainly the third power t^3 cannot be expressed as a spatial quantity at all. In purely mathematical spatial quantities, it is only after I have obtained the third power that I get outside of ordinary space, but in this other case I am probably already outside of our space in the case of the second power and in the third not in space at all anymore.

Therefore you must realize that you have to conceive of t as entirely different in its nature from spatial quantities. You must consider t as something already squared, as a second power, and the squared t you must think of as of the third power, the cubed t as of the fourth power. This takes us out of our ordinary space. Consider now how this gives our formula a very special aspect.

For the last member of this formula forces me to go out of three-dimensional space. In such a case, even when I confine myself to simple calculation I must go beyond three-dimensional space for the last member of the formula. I state this purely hypothetically, as a possibility, as is customary in mathematical formulas.

When you observe a triangle and determine that it has three angles, you are dealing, at the start, with a conceived triangle. Since merely thinking about it is not enough to satisfy your senses, you draw it, but the drawing adds nothing to your idea. You have as a given that the sum of the angles is 180 degrees or – in a right-angled triangle – that the square of the hypotenuse equals the sum of the squares of the other two sides. These things are handled as I am now handling the power of t.

Let us now go back and see what we have established as fact. This is the way it is done in geometry. When I observe an actual triangle in bridge construction or elsewhere, the abstract idea verifies itself. What I have thought of in the abstract t has at first a similarity with melting and evaporating. (We will gradually get nearer to the essence of the reality.) I could not express melting and evaporating in terms of the three dimensions of space. The only way I could force them into the curve was to stop and then continue again. In order to prove the hypothesis that I made for you, it was necessary, in the case of the third power, the cube of the temperature, to go outside of three-dimensional space.

I am showing you how we must break a path, as it were, if we wish to place together those phenomena that simply by being put side by side illustrate the being of heat and enable us to attain an understanding similar to that reached in the preceding course of lectures on light.

The physicist Crookes[13] approached this subject from entirely different hypotheses. It is significant that his considerations led him to a result similar to the one we have arrived at merely hypothetically and whose validity we will establish in the next lectures. He also concluded that temperature changes had essentially to do with a kind of fourth dimension in space. It is important at this time to pay attention to these things, because the relativists, with Einstein at their head, feel obliged when they go outside of three-dimensional space to consider time as the fourth dimension. Thus in the Einstein formulae, one always finds time as the fourth dimension. Crookes, on the other hand, considered the gain or loss of heat as the fourth dimension. So much for this sidelight on historical development.

Now add to these phenomena what I have formerly emphasized. I have said that an ordinary solid may be handled, and it will keep its form. That is, it has a definite boundary. A fluid must be poured into a vessel, It always forms a flat upper surface, and the rest takes the shape of the vessel. This is not so for a gas or vapor, which expands in every direction. In order to hold it, I must put it into a vessel closed on all sides. This totally enclosed vessel gives the gas its form, so that a gas has form only if enclosed on all sides. The solid body possesses a form simply by virtue of the fact that it is a solid body. It has a form in itself, as it were. Considering the fluid as an intermediate condition, we will note that the solid and gaseous bodies may be described as opposites. The solid body provides for itself that which I must add to the gaseous body, namely the completely surrounding boundary.

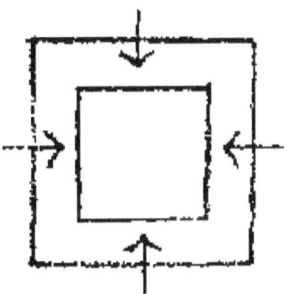

Now, however, a peculiar thing occurs in the case of a gas. When you put a gas into a smaller vessel (see drawing), using the same amount of gas but contracting the walls all around, you must use pressure. You have to exert pressure. This means nothing other than that you have to overcome the pressure of the gas. You do it by exerting pressure on the walls that give form to the gas. We may state the matter thus, that a gas which has the tendency to spread out in all directions is held together by the resistance of the containing walls. This resistance is there by itself in the case of the solid body. Thus without any theorizing, but simply keeping in mind the quite obvious facts, I can define a polar contrast between a gas and a solid body in the following way: what I must add to the gas from the outside is present by itself in the solid. But now, if you cool the gas, you can pass back again to the boiling point and get a liquid from the vapor, and if you cool it further to the melting point, you can get the solid from the liquid. That is to say, you are able by processes connected with the being of warmth to bring about a condition in which you no longer have to build the form from the outside, but the creation of form takes place by itself from within. Since I have done nothing but bring about a change in the heat condition, it is self-evident that form is related in some way to changes in the heat state. In a solid, something is present that is not present in a gas. If we hold a wall up against a solid, the solid does not by itself exert pressure against the wall unless we ourselves bring this about. When, however, we enclose a gas in a vessel, the gas presses against the solid wall. You see, we come upon the concept of pressure and have to bring this creation of pressure into relation with the heat condition. We have to say to ourselves that it is necessary to find a certain relation between the form of solid bodies, the diffusing tendency of gases, and the opposition of the boundary walls that oppose this diffusion. When we seek this relation, we can hope really to press forward into the nature of the connection between heat and corporeality.

Lecture IV

*Stuttgart,
March 4, 1920*

You will perhaps have noticed in our considerations here that we are striving for a particular goal. We are trying to place together a series of phenomena from the realm of heat in such a way that the real nature of warmth becomes obvious to us from these phenomena. We have become acquainted in a general way with certain relationships among phenomena within the realm of heat, and in particular we have observed the relationship of this realm to the ability of substances to expand. We have then followed this with an attempt to picture to ourselves the nature of form in solid bodies, fluids, and gaseous bodies. I have also spoken of the relationship of heat to changes produced in bodies when they pass from the solid to the fluid and from the fluid to the gaseous or vaporous condition.

Now I wish to present to you certain relationships that come up when we have to do with gases or vapors. We already know that these are connected with heat, since by means of heat we bring about the gaseous condition, and again, by appropriate change of temperature, that we can obtain a liquid from a gas. Now you know that when we have a solid body, we cannot by any means interpenetrate this solid with another. The observation of such simple, elementary relationships is of enormous importance if we really wish to penetrate through to the nature of heat. The experiment I will carry out now will show that water vapor produced here in this vessel passes into this second vessel. And now having filled the second vessel with water vapor, we will gradually produce in the first vessel another vapor whose formation you can see by reason of the fact that it is colored.[14] You see that in spite of our having filled the vessel with water vapor, the other vapor goes into the space filled with the water vapor. That is, one gas does not prevent another gas from penetrating the space it occupies. We may express this by saying that gaseous or vaporous bodies may to a certain extent interpenetrate each other.

I will now show you another phenomenon that will illustrate another relationship of heat to certain facts. In the left-hand

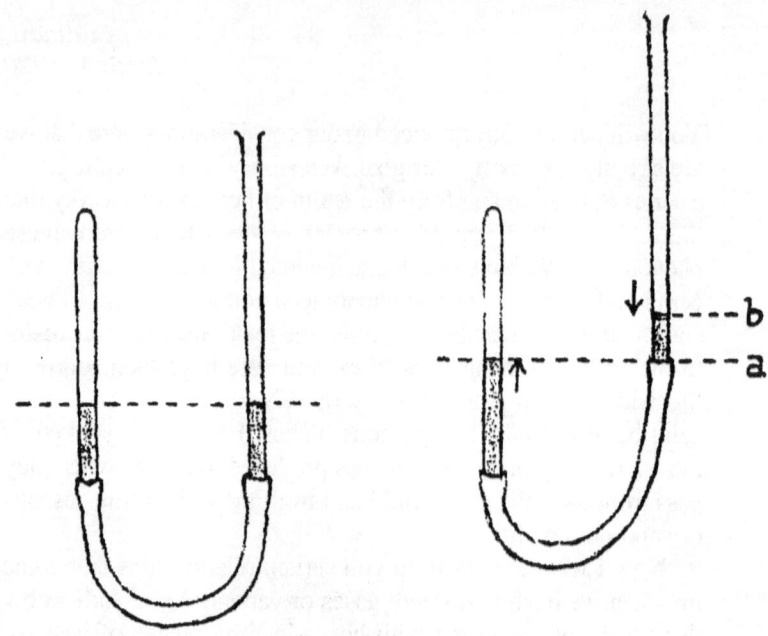

tube, we have air that is in equilibrium with the outer air with which we are always surrounded. I must remind you that this outer air surrounding us is always under a certain pressure, the usual atmospheric pressure, and it exerts this pressure on us. Thus we can say that the air inside the left-hand tube is under the same pressure as the outer air itself, which is shown by the similar level of the mercury column in the right- and left-hand tubes. You can see that on both the right- and left-hand sides, the mercury column is at the same height (see drawing, left), and that since here on the right the tube is open to the atmosphere the air in the closed tube is at atmospheric pressure. We will now alter the conditions by bringing pressure on the air in the left-hand tube. We can do this by lifting the right tube and thus adding to the left tube the pressure that results from the increased level of the mercury column (see drawing, right). By doing this we have added to the usual atmospheric pressure the pressure due to the higher mercury column. That is, we have simply added the weight of the mercury from here to here (see drawing, from *a* to *b*). By thus increasing the pressure exerted on this air by the pressure corresponding to the weight of the mercury column, the volume of the air in the left-hand tube is, as you can see, made smaller. We can therefore say that when we increase the pressure on a gas its volume decreases. We must now extend this observation and consider it a general phenomenon that the space occupied by a gas and the pressure exerted on it have an inverse ratio to each other. The greater the pressure the smaller the volume, and the greater the volume the smaller must be the pressure acting on the gas. We can express this in the form of an equation where the volume V_1 is related to the volume V_2 as the pressure P_2 is related to the pressure P_1:

$$V_1 : V_2 = P_2 : P_1$$

from which it follows that:

$$V_1 P_1 = V_2 P_2$$

This expresses a relatively general law (we can always speak only of relative laws and will see why later). This may be stated as follows: volume and pressure of gases are related in such a way that the volume-pressure product is a constant at constant temperature. As we have said, such phenomena as these must be placed side by side if we are to approach the nature of heat. And now, since our considerations are to be thought of as a basis for education, we must consider the matter from two aspects. On the one hand we must build up a knowledge of the method of thinking of modern physics and on the other hand we must throw aside certain obstacles that modern physics places in the path of a real understanding of the nature of heat.

Please picture vividly to yourselves that when we consider the nature of heat we are necessarily dealing at the same time with volume increases, that is, with changes in space and with changes of pressure. In other words, mechanical facts meet us in our consideration of heat. I have to speak of these things in detail repeatedly, although it is not customary to do this. Space changes, pressure changes – mechanical facts meet us.

For the development of modern physics, the facts that meet us when we consider heat are purely and simply mechanical facts. These mechanical occurrences are the milieu, as it were, in which heat is observed. The being of heat is left, so to speak, in the realm of the unknown, and attention is focused on the mechanical processes that play themselves out under its influence. Since the perception of heat is alleged to be a purely subjective thing, the expansion of mercury accompanying a change of heat condition or sensation of heat is considered as something belonging in the realm of the mechanical. The dependence of gas pressure, for instance, on the temperature, which we will consider further, is thought of as essentially mechanical, and the being of heat is left out of consideration. We saw yesterday that there is a good reason for this, for when we attempt to calculate heat, difficulties arise in the usual calculations and we cannot, for example, handle the third power of the temperature in the same way as the third power of an ordinary quantity in space. And since modern physics has not appreciated the importance of the higher powers of the temperature, it has simply stricken them out of the expansion formulae I mentioned to you in the previous lectures.

Now you need only consider the following: in the sphere of outer nature heat always appears in external mechanical processes, primarily in space processes. Space processes are there to begin with, and in them the heat appears. It is this that constrains us to think of heat as we do of lines in space and that leads us to proceed from the first power of expansion in space to the second power of expansion.

When we observe the first power of the expansion, the line, and we wish to go over to the second power, we have to go off of the line. That is, we must add a second dimension to the first. The standard of measurement of the second power has to be thought of as entirely different from that of the first power. We have to proceed in an entirely similar fashion when we consider a temperature condition. The first power is present in the expansion, so to speak. Change of temperature and expansion are

related in such a way that they may be expressed by a rectilinear coordinate system (see drawing). When I wish to make a graph representing change in expansion with change in temperature, I am obliged to add the axis of abscissa to the ordinate. But this makes it necessary to consider what is appearing as temperature not as a first power but as a second power, and the second power as a third. When we deal with the third power of the temperature, we can no longer stay in our ordinary space. This simple consideration, dealing, it is true, with rather subtle distinctions, will show you that when we have to do with heat manifesting itself as the third power we cannot limit ourselves to the three dimensions of space. It will show you how we are obliged, when we deal with the third power in so far as heat effects are concerned, to go out of space.

Modern physics sets itself the task of explaining the phenomena while remaining within three-dimensional space. And in setting themselves this task, physicists have ensured that they will pass over the real nature of warmth, since it cannot be found within three-dimensional space. They can get a hold of the nature of warmth only through its manifestations in three-dimensional space. You see, here we have a very important point where physical science has to cross a kind of Rubicon to reach a higher view of the world. It is necessary to emphasize the fact that since so little attempt is made to attain clarity on this point, a corresponding lack enters into the comprehensive worldview emerging from this viewpoint.

Imagine that physicists presented these matters to their students in such a way as to show that one must simply leave ordinary space in which mechanical phenomena are at work when heat phenomena are to be observed. If they did this, these physics teachers would call forth in their students – who are most likely intelligent people since they find themselves able to study the subject – the idea that a person cannot really know the reality of physics without leaving three-dimensional space. Then it would be much easier to present people with a higher world view. For people in general, even if they were not students of physics, would say, "We cannot form a judgment on the matter, but those who have studied know that the human being must rise through the physics of space to relationships other than purely spatial relationships." Therefore so much depends on physics receiving ideas like the ones presented in our considerations here. This would help spread a worldview with a spiritual basis among people, a view quite different from the one held today. The physicist explains all phenomena exclusively by means of mechanical facts in space – then life must also be a mechanical thing, soul processes must be mechanical, and spiritual things must also be mechanical. Strict science wants to know nothing of any spiritual foundations of the world, and it exerts an especially powerful authority because people are not well versed in it. What people are well acquainted with, they generally pass their own judgment on and do not permit others to be the authorities. What they do not know well they accept on authority. If more were done to popularize the so-called "strictly exact science," the authority of some of those who sit entrenched in possession of this "exact science" would practically disappear.

During the course of the nineteenth century, another fact was added to the facts we have already observed, a fact about which I have spoken briefly. This is that mechanical processes not only appear in connection with the phenomena of heat but that heat can be transformed into mechanical processes. You see such a process in the ordinary steam locomotive in which heat is applied and forward motion results. Other mechanical processes, friction and the like, can be transformed back into heat since the mechanical processes, as it is said, bring about the appearance of heat. Thus mechanical processes and heat processes may be mutually transformed into each other.

We will sketch these relationships today in a preliminary way and go into the details pertaining to this realm in subsequent lectures. It has been found further that not only heat but also electrical and chemical processes may be changed into mechanical processes. Out of this has been developed what was called during the nineteenth century the "mechanical theory of heat."

The principal postulate of this mechanical theory of heat is that heat and mechanical effects are mutually convertible into one another. Now suppose we consider this idea somewhat more closely. We must first consider these somewhat elementary aspects in the realm of physics. If we overlook the elementary aspects in our basic consideration, we will have to give up attaining any clarity in the realm of heat. We must therefore ask the question – what does it really mean when I say: heat as it is applied in the steam engine generates outer motion, and therefore outer mechanical work? What does it mean when I transform this idea into the conclusion that through heat mechanical work is produced in the external world? Let us distinguish clearly between what we can establish as fact and the ideas we add to these facts. We can establish the fact that a heat process is subsequently revealed by mechanical work, by a mechanical process. Then the conclusion is drawn that the heat process, the heat as such, has been changed into the mechanical process, into mechanical work.

If I come into this room and find that I am comfortable with the room's temperature, I may think to myself, perhaps unconsciously, without saying it in words: in this room it is comfortable. I sit down at the desk and write something. Then following the same course of reasoning as has given rise to the mechanical theory of heat, I would say: I came into the room, the heat condition influenced me, and what I wrote down is a consequence of this heat condition. Speaking from a certain point of view I might say that if I had found the place cold like a cellar I would have hurried out and would not have done the work of writing. If I now add to the above fact the conclusion that the heat conducted to me has been changed into the work I did, then I have obviously left something out of my thinking. I have left out everything that can take place only through myself. If I am to comprehend the whole reality, I must include everything I have left out in drawing my conclusion.

The question now arises: when the corresponding conclusion is drawn in the realm of heat, by assuming that the motion of the locomotive is simply the transformed heat from the boiler, have I not fallen into the error noted above? That is, have I not committed the same fallacy as when I speak of a transformation of heat into an effect that can only take place because I myself am part of the picture? It may appear to be trivial to direct attention to a thing such as this, but it is just these trivialities that have been completely forgotten in the entire mechanical theory of heat. What is more, enormously important things result from this. Two things need to be related to one another here. First, in the moment when we pass from the mechanical realm into the realm where heat is active, we really have to leave three-dimensional space; secondly, we have to consider that when external nature is observed, we simply do not have that which is interpolated in the case where heat is transformed into my writing. When heat is changed into my writing, I can note from observation of my external bodily nature that something has been interpolated in the process. Suppose, however, that I simply consider the fact that I must leave three-dimensional space in order to relate the transformation of heat into mechanical effects. Then I can say that perhaps the most important factor involved in this change plays its part outside of three-dimensional space. In the example I gave you, which concerned myself, the manner in which I entered into the process took place outside of three dimensions. And when I speak of simple transformation of heat into work, I am guilty of the same superficiality as when I consider transformation of heat into a piece of written work and leave myself out.

This, however, leads to a very significant universal consequence, for it requires me to experience myself as being led in external nature, even in lifeless, inorganic nature, into a being that does not express itself in three-dimensional space, which is active, so to speak, from behind three-dimensional space. This is fundamental in relation to our observations of the nature of heat itself.

Since we have outlined the elementary aspects of our conception of the realm of heat, we may look back again on something we have already indicated, namely on man's own relation to heat. We may compare the perception of heat to perception in other realms. I have already called attention to the fact that when we perceive light, for instance, we note this perception of light and color to be bound up with special organs. These organs are simply inserted into our body, and we cannot therefore speak of being related to color and light with our whole organism; our relation to it concerns only a part of our organism. Likewise with acoustical or sound phenomena, we are related to them with a portion of our organism, namely the organ of hearing. To the being of heat we are related through our entire organism. This fact conditions our relationship to the being of heat. And when we look more closely, when we try, as it were, to express these facts in terms of human knowledge, we are obliged to say that we ourselves are really this heat being. In so far as we are human beings moving around in space, we are ourselves this heat being. Imagine the temperature were to be raised a couple of hundred degrees: we would be unable to be identical with that temperature state. It would be similar if we were to consider the temperature lowered by a hundred degrees. Thus the heat condition belongs to that within which we are continually living, which we experience as a matter of fact but do not take into our consciousness. Only when some deviation from the normal condition occurs do we become conscious of it in some form.

Another fact may be connected with this one. It is this. You may say to yourselves when you touch a warm object and perceive the heat condition by means of your organism that you do it with the tip of your tongue, with the tip of your finger, or you can do it with other parts of your organism – with the lobes of your ears, let us say. In fact, you can perceive the heat condition with your entire organism. But there is something else you can perceive with your entire organism. You can perceive anything exerting pressure upon your organism. And here again, you are not limited strictly as you are in the case of the eye and color perception to a certain member of your entire organism. It would be very convenient if our heads, at least, were an exception to this rule of pressure perception – a rap on the head would not make us so uncomfortable then! We can say that there is an inner kinship between the nature of our relationship to the outer world perceived as heat and perceived as pressure. We have today spoken of pressure-volume relations. We come back now to our own organism and find an inner kinship between our relationship to heat and to pressure. Such a fact must be considered as a groundwork for what will follow.

There is something else, however, that must be taken into account as a preliminary to further observations. You know that in the most popular textbooks of physiology a good deal of emphasis is laid on the fact that we have certain bodily organs by means of which we perceive the usual sense qualities. We have the eye for color, the ear for sound, the organ of taste for certain chemical processes, etc. Over our entire organism is spread out the unified heat organ, as it was, and also the unified pressure organ. Now, usually attention is drawn to the fact that there are certain other things of which we are aware but for which we have no organs: magnetism and electricity are perceived by us only through their effects and stand, as it were, outside of us, not immediately perceived. It is said sometimes that if we imagined that our eyes were electrically sensitive instead of light sensitive, then when we turned them toward a telegraph wire we would perceive the streaming electricity in it – electricity would be known not merely by its effects but, like light and color, would be immediately perceived. We cannot do this. We must therefore say that electricity is an example of something for whose immediate perception we have no organ. Thus there are aspects of nature for which we have organs of perception and aspects of nature for which we do not have organs – at least this is what is said in the physiology textbooks.

The question is whether a more unbiased observer might not come to a different conclusion from those whose view is expressed above. You all know that what we call our ordinary passive concepts through which we apprehend the world are closely bound up with the impressions received through the eye, the ear, and somewhat less so through taste and smell impressions. If you simply consider language, you may draw from it the summation of your conceptual life, and you will become aware that the words used to represent our ideas are residues of our higher sense impressions. Even when we speak the very abstract word "*Sein*" (being), the derivation is from "*Ich habe gesehen,*" (I have seen). What I have seen I can speak of as possessing "being." In "being" there is included "What has been seen." Now without becoming completely materialistic (and we will see later why it is not necessary to become so), it may be said that our conceptual world is really a kind of residue of seeing and hearing and to a lesser extent of smelling and tasting. (These last two enter less into our conceptual world.) Through the intimate connection between our consciousness and our higher sense impressions, our consciousness is enabled to take up the higher passive conceptual world.

But from another side there comes into the soul nature the will, and you remember how I have often told you in these anthroposophical lectures that the human being is really asleep as far as his will is concerned. He is, properly considered, awake only in his higher passive conceptual realm. What you will, you perceive only through these ideas or concepts. You have the idea: I will raise this glass. Now, in so far as your mental act contains ideas, it is a residue of outer sense perceptions. You place before yourself in thought something that belongs entirely in the realm of the seen; even when you think of it, you have an image of something seen. Such an immediately derived image you cannot create from a will process proper, from what happens when you stretch out your arm and actually grasp the glass with your hand and raise it. That act is entirely outside of your consciousness. You are not aware of what happens between your consciousness and the delicate processes in your arm. Our unconsciousness of it is as complete as our unconsciousness between falling asleep and awaking. But something is really there and takes place, and can its existence be denied simply because we do not perceive these processes?

These processes must be intimately bound up with us as human beings because, after all, it is we who raise the glass. In considering our human nature we are thus led from what is immediately alive in consciousness to will processes taking place, as it were, outside of consciousness. Imagine that everything above this line (see drawing) is in the realm of consciousness. What is underneath is in the realm of will and is outside of consciousness. Starting from this point, we proceed to the outer phenomena of nature and find our eye intimately connected with color phenomena, something that we can consciously apprehend; we find our ear intimately connected with sound, as some-

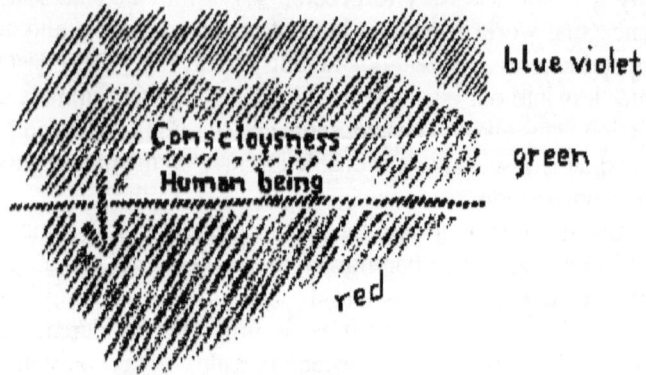

thing we can consciously apprehend. Tasting and smelling, however, are apprehended in a more dreamlike way. Here we have something that is in the realm of consciousness and yet is intimately bound up with the outer world.

If we now go to magnetic and electrical phenomena, the entity that is active in these is withdrawn from us in contrast with those phenomena of nature that have immediate connection with us through our organs. This entity escapes us. Therefore the physicists and physiologists say that we have no organ for it; it is cut off from us. It lies outside us (see drawing, above). We have a realm that we approach when we draw near the outer world. There we have light phenomena and heat phenomena. How do electrical phenomena escape us? We can trace no connection between them and any of our organs. Within us we have the residues of our working through light and sound phenomena in the form of our ideas. When we move downward, however (see drawing above, red), our own being disappears from us into will.

I will now tell you something a bit paradoxical, but think it over until tomorrow. Imagine we were not living human beings but living rainbows and that with our consciousness we dwelt in the green portion of the spectrum. On the one side we would trail off into the blue-violet with our unconsciousness. This would elude us on one side, like electricity. On the other side we would trail off into the yellow and red, and this would elude us like our will within. If we were rainbows, we would not perceive green, because what we are we do not perceive immediately; we experience it. We would touch the border of our own inner being when we tried, as it were, to pass from the green to the yellow. We would say: "I, a rainbow, approach my red portion, which I can no longer perceive as something inner; I approach my blue-violet portion, but it eludes me. I am in the middle." If we were thinking, living rainbows, we would live in this way in the green and have on the one side a blue-violet pole and on the other side a yellow-red pole. Similarly, as human beings we are placed with our consciousness between the qualities of nature that elude us on one side, like magnetism and electricity, and the inner qualities that elude us on the other, like the phenomena of will.

Lecture V

*Stuttgart,
March 5, 1920*

I would have liked to carry out some experiments for you today that could round out the series of facts we need to lead us to our goal. It is not possible to do so today, however, and I must accordingly arrange my lecture somewhat differently from the way I intended. The reason for this is partly that the necessary apparatus is not in working order and partly that we lack alcohol today, just as yesterday we lacked ice.

We will therefore take up in more detail the matters we began to consider yesterday. I will ask you to consider all the facts that were presented to you in order to gain a survey of the relationships of various bodies to the being of heat. You will realize that certain typical phenomena meet us so that we can say that in these phenomena there is the expression of certain relations involving the being of heat, which remains unknown to us at first.[15] Examples are the relationship of heat to pressure exerted on a body or the state of aggregation that a body assumes according to its temperature, also the extent of space occupied, the volume. On the one hand we are able to see how a solid body melts, and we can establish the fact that during the melting of the solid no rise in temperature is measurable by the thermometer or any other temperature-measuring instrument. The temperature increase stands still, as it were, during the melting.

If we then study a fluid we discover that with increased heat it expands again under the influence of the application of heat (*Wärmezufuhr*). On the other hand, we can see the change from a liquid to a gas, and there again we find the disappearance of the temperature increase and its reappearance when the whole body has passed into the gaseous condition. These facts make up a series that you can demonstrate for yourselves and that you can follow with your eyes, your senses, and with instruments. Yesterday we also called attention to certain inner experiences of the human being himself that he has under the influence of warmth and also under the influence of other sense qualities such as light and tone. But we saw that outer processes such as magnetism and electricity do not produce real sense impressions, at least not immediate sense impressions, because, as ordinary physics says, the human being has no sense organ for these entities. We say, indeed, that we come to know electrical and magnetic properties through determining their effects, the attraction of an object to a magnet, for instance, and the many effects of electrical processes. But we have no immediate sense perception of electricity and magnetism as we have for tone and light.

We then noted particularly, and this must be emphasized, that our own passive concepts, by which we represent the world, are really a kind of distillation of the higher sense impressions. Wherever you examine this question, you will find these higher concepts and will be able to convince yourselves that they are ultimately the distilled essence of the higher sense impressions. I illustrated this yesterday in the case of the concept of being. You can discern echoes of tone in the designations of the higher concepts, and shining through everywhere you can see what these concepts have borrowed from light. But there is one kind of concept with which you cannot do this, as you will soon see. You cannot do it in the realm of mathematical concepts. In so far as they are purely mathematical, there is no trace of the tonal or the visible.

Now we must not deceive ourselves here. Man immediately thinks of tone when he speaks of the wave number of sound vibrations. Of course I am not referring to this sort of thing. I mean everything that is obtained from mathematical concepts, from pure mathematics: for instance, the content of Pythagoras' theorem, or that the sum of the angles of a triangle is 180 degrees, or that the whole is greater than its parts, etc. The basis of these pure mathematical concepts is not related to the seen or the heard, but it relates itself in the last analysis to our will impulse. Strange as it may seem to you at first, you will always find this fact when you really look at these things from the psychological point of view, as it were. The person who draws a triangle (the drawn triangle is only an externalization) is attaining in concept the unfolding of his will around the three angles. There is an unfolding of action around three angles as shown by the motion of the hand or by walking, by turning of the body. What you have within you as a will concept is in reality what you carry into the pure mathematical concept. This is, in fact, the essential distinction between mathematical concepts and other concepts. This is the distinction about which Kant[16] and other philosophers racked their heads so intensively. You can distinguish the inner compelling nature of mathematical concepts from the merely empirical or noncompelling nature of other concepts. This distinction arises from the fact that mathematical concepts are so closely bound up with our own selves that we carry our will nature into them. Only what we experience in the sphere of the will is brought into mathematical operations. This is what makes them seem so certain to us. What is not felt to be so intimately bound up with us, but is simply felt through an organ placed in a certain part of us, appears uncertain and empirical. This is the real distinction.

Now, I must call your attention to a certain fact. When we dip down into the sphere of the will, from which emerge the abstractions that make up the sum of our pure arithmetical and geometrical concepts, we enter the unknown region of the will, which takes its course in our organs, a region as unknown to us inwardly as electricity and magnetism are outwardly. Yesterday I tried to illustrate this by asking you to imagine yourselves as living, thinking rainbows with your consciousness in the green, in consequence of which you would not perceive the green but would perceive the colors on each side of it, fading into the unknown. I compared the red to dipping down inwardly into the unknown sphere of the will and the blue-violet to the outward extension into the spheres of electricity and magnetism and the like.

At this point in our course I am inserting this psychological-physiological point of view, as it might be called, because it is essential for the future of physics that people be led back again to the relationship of the human being to physical observations. Unless this relationship to the human being is established, the confusion that reigns in physics at present cannot be eliminated. We will see this as we pursue further the phenomena of heat. But it is not so easy to establish this relationship to man in the thinking of today. The reason for this is that modern man cannot easily bridge the gap between what he perceives outwardly as phenomena in space, as outer sense phenomena, and what he experiences within. In these modern times there is such a pronounced dualism between everything we experience as knowledge of the outer world and what we experience inwardly that it is extraordinarily difficult to bridge this gap. But the gap must be bridged if physics is to advance. To accomplish this, we must use the intuitive faculties rather than the rational when we relate something external to what goes on within man himself. Thus we can begin to grasp how we must orient ourselves in observing physical phenomena as important as those arising from heat.

Let me call your attention now to the following. Suppose you learn a poem by heart. As you learn it, you will first find it necessary to become acquainted with the ideas underlying the poem. At first when you recite the poem you will always have the tendency to let these ideas unfold in your mind. The more frequently you recite the poem, however, especially when there is a lapse of time between the recitations, the less intensely you are obliged to think of the ideas. There may come a time when it is not necessary to think at all but you are able simply to reel off the recitation mechanically. We never actually reach this point – we do not wish to do so, in fact – but we approach the condition asymptotically, as it were. Our feelings as human beings prevent us from reaching this stage of purely mechanical repetition, but it is conceivable that we could get to the point at which we would not need to think at all, that when we spoke the first line the rest of the poem would follow without any thinking about it. You may recognize the similarity between such a condition and the approach of the hyperbola to its asymptotes. But this leads us to the conception that when we recite a poem we are dealing with two different activities working simultaneously in our organism. We are dealing with a mechanical reeling-off of certain processes of our organization, and along with this go the processes included in our soul concepts. On the one hand, we have what we can properly speak of as playing itself out outwardly and mechanically in space, and on the other hand we have a soul process that is entirely nonspatial in nature.

Focus your attention now just on what reels itself off mechanically, physically; you can do this in thought, for instance, if you imagine you recited a poem in a foreign language that you didn't understand – then you have simply a mechanical, physical process. The instant you accompany this mechanical process with thinking, you have an inner soul activity that cannot be brought out into space. You cannot express in space the thinking with which a person accompanies the recitation, whereas you can do so with the mechanical processes of actual speaking, of pronouncing words.

Let me give you an analogy now. When we follow the heating of a solid body to the moment it reaches its melting point, the temperature is always getting higher. We can see this on the thermometer. When the solid begins to melt, the thermometer stands still until the melting is complete. Once the melting point is complete the thermometer rises again. It is impossible, to begin with, to pursue with the thermometer what happens to the heat while the solid is melting. There is an analogy between what we can follow outwardly with the thermometer, the outer physical process, and what we can follow physically in the spoken word. And there is also an analogy between what eludes us and lies in the concepts of the reciter and what happens to the heat while the melting is going on. Here, you see, we have an example where we can, by analogy at least, bridge the gap between an outer observation and something in the human being. In realms of human activity other than that of speech we do not have such ready examples to bridge the gap. This is because in speech there is on the one hand the conceivable possibility that a person could mechanically recite something learned by heart; on the other hand there is the possibility that the person would not speak at all but simply think about it and thus remove it entirely from the realm of space. In other spheres we do not have the opportunity to make this distinction and see precisely how one activity passes over into another. This is especially difficult when we wish to pursue the nature of heat, because we have to set out to investigate physiologically and psychologically how heat behaves when we have taken it into ourselves.

Yesterday, by way of illustration, I said to you: "I go into a room that is comfortably heated. I sit down and write something." I cannot so easily find the connection between what I experience or feel when I go into the warm room and what takes place in me inwardly when I write down my thoughts. I cannot determine the connection so readily as I can between reciting something and thinking about it inwardly. Thus it is difficult to find through inner experience something that corresponds to the outer experience of warmth. But it is a question of gradually approaching the concepts that will lead us further in this direction, and in this connection I want to call your attention to something you know from anthroposophy.

When we make the attempt to extend our thinking by meditation, to increase its inner intensity, we work with our thoughts in such a way that again and again we reach the condition where we know we are using soul forces without the help of the body.[17] You know that in order to do this our entire inner soul life has to change. With ordinary abstract thoughts man cannot enter the higher region of human soul life. There thoughts become picture-like, and they have to be translated out of the imaginative element into our abstract element if they are to be communicated to those who are unfamiliar with the imaginative element. But you only need understand a method of looking at these things such as is presented, for instance, in my book, *An Outline of Spiritual Science*. In this book, I attempted to be as true to the facts as possible, and this is what has so disturbed the people who are only able to think abstractly. For the attempt must be made to translate things into picture form, as I had to do to an extreme extent in the description of the Saturn and Sun states. There you will find purely pictorial concepts mixed in with the others. It is very hard for people to go over into the pictures, because these things can no longer be put into the abstract form. The reason for this is that when we think abstractly, when we move within the narrow confines of concepts, in which people today are so much at home, especially in the realm of natural science, we are using ideas completely dependent on our bodies. We cannot do without our bodies, for instance, when we set out to think through the things set forth as physical laws in the physics books. There we must think in such a way that we use our bodies as instruments. When we rise to the sphere of the imagination, then the abstract ideas must be completely altered, because our inner soul life no longer uses the physical body.

You may now take what I might call a comprehensive view of the realm of imaginative thinking. This realm of imaginative thinking in us has nothing to do with what is bound up in our outer corporeality. We rise to a region where we live as beings of soul and spirit without dependence on our outer corporeality. In other words, the instant we enter the realm of the imaginative, we leave space. We are then no longer in space.

This has an extremely important consequence. In the previous course[18] I made a very strong differentiation between mere kinematics and what enters into our consideration as the mechanical, such as mass, for instance. As long as I consider only kinematics, I need only think of things. I can write them down on a blackboard or a sheet of paper and complete the survey of motion and space as far as my thinking takes me. But in that case I must remain within what can be surveyed in terms of time and space. Why is this? There is a very definite reason for this. You must be very clear about the following: all human beings, as they exist on earth, are like you yourselves within time and space. They are bounded by a definite space and are related as spatial objects to other spatial objects. When you speak of space, therefore, considering the matter in an unprejudiced way, you are unable to take the Kantian ideas seriously. For if space were inside us, then we ourselves could not be within space. We only think space is inside of us. We can free ourselves of this fancy, of this notion, if we consider the fact that this being-within-space has a very real meaning for us. If space were inside of us, it would have no significance for a person whether he were born in Moscow or Vienna. But where we are born has a very real significance. As a terrestrial-empirical person, I am completely a product of spatial facts. That is, as a human being, I belong to relations that form themselves in space. It is the same with time. You would all be different people if you had been born twenty years earlier. That is to say, your life does not have time inside of it, but time has your life within it. Thus as empirical persons you stand within time and space. And when we talk of time and space, or when we express our will impulses pictorially, as I have explained we do in geometry, this is because we ourselves live inside of spatial and temporal relations and are therefore quite definitely related to them and so are able, *a priori*, to speak of them as we do in mathematics.

When you go over to the concept of mass, this is not so. The matter must then be put in a different way. In respect to mass, you are dealing with something quite special. You cannot say that you cut out a portion of time or space but rather that you live in the general space or the general time. But when you eat or drink, you take something from the general mass and make it into your own mass. This mass, then, is within you. It cannot be denied that this mass with all its activities, all of its potentialities, is active *inside* of you; at this moment it falls into a different category from time and space. It is precisely because you yourself take part with your inner being, as it were, in the properties of the mass, because you take it up into your being, that it does not allow itself to be brought into consciousness like time and space. In the realm where the world gives us our own substance, we thus enter unknown regions. This is related to the fact that our will is, for instance, very dependent on the processes of mass inside us. But we are unconscious of these processes of mass; we are asleep to them. And we are related to a process of mass in us, while our will is active, in the same way that we relate to the world in general between going asleep and awaking. We are not conscious of either one. For human consciousness there is no immediate distinction between them.

Thus we gradually bring these things nearer to the human being. The physicists tend to shy away from this attempt to bring such things near to the human being. But we can obtain really reasonable concepts in no other way than by developing a relationship between the human being and the world, a relationship that does not exist at the start, as in the case of time and space. We speak of time and space, let us say, out of our rational faculties, from which comes the certainty of the mathematical and kinematical sciences.[19] Of things experienced merely outwardly through the senses – things related to mass – we can speak at first only through experience. But we can analyze the relationship between the activity of a portion of mass within us and outer mass activity. As soon as we do this, we can begin to deal with mass in the same way that we deal with the obvious relationship between ourselves and time or ourselves and space. This means that in our physical concepts we must grow inwardly into a relationship to the world such as we have for mathematical or kinematical concepts.

It is a peculiar thing that, as we become independent of our own bodies, in which all those things take place to which we are asleep, such as will impulses, as we raise ourselves to imaginative concepts, we really take a step nearer the world. We are always approaching more nearly that which otherwise rules in us unconsciously. There is no other way to gain access to the objectivity of the facts than to push forward with our own inner soul development. At the same time that we detach ourselves from our own materiality, we approach more and more closely what is going on in the outside world.

It is not so easy, however, to obtain even the most elementary experiences in this realm, since a person must transform himself in such a way that he pays attention to things that are not noticed at all under ordinary circumstances. But now I will tell you something that will probably astonish you greatly. Let us suppose you have advanced a little further on the path of imaginative thinking. Suppose you have really begun to think imaginatively. You will then experience something that will astonish you: it will be much easier than it formerly was for you to recite in a merely mechanical way a poem that you have learned by heart. It will not be more difficult for you, but less so. If you examine your soul without prejudice and with care, you will at once find that you are more prone to recite a poem mechanically without thinking about it if you have undergone a spiritual training than if you have not undergone such a training. You do not dislike slipping into the mechanical as strongly as you did before the spiritual development. It is things like this that are not usually stated outright but are meant when it is said over and over that the experiences you have in spiritual training are really opposed to the concepts you would ordinarily have before entering an spiritual training. Thus when the more advanced stage is reached, one comes to observe more easily the ideas of ordinary life. Anyone who advances in spiritual development is therefore exposed to the danger of becoming afterward a greater materialist than before. An orderly spiritual training guards against this, but the tendency to become materialistic is quite marked in the very people who have undergone spiritual development. I will tell you why this is so by means of an example.

You see, in ordinary life what the theorists maintain is really the case: the brain thinks. But ordinarily a person does not actually perceive this fact. It is quite possible in this ordinary life to carry out a dialogue such as I did in my childhood with a friend who was a crass materialist and became more and more so.[20] He would say, "When I think my brain does the thinking." I would say to that, "Yes, but when you are with me you always say *I* will do this, *I* think. Why don't you say, *my brain* will do this, my brain thinks? You are always lying!" The reason for this is that for the theoretical materialist, quite naturally, there is no possibility of observing the processes in the brain. He cannot observe these physical processes. Therefore, materialism remains for him merely a theory.

The moment a person advances somewhat from imaginative to inspirational ideas, he becomes able really to observe the parallel processes in the brain. Then what goes on in the material part of the brain becomes really visible. Aside from the fact that it is extremely seductive, the things a person can observe in his own activity appear to him more and more wonderful, for this activity of the brain can be observed as something much more wonderful than all that the theoretical materialists can describe about it. The temptation thus arises to become ever more materialistic for the very reason that the activity of the human brain has become observable. Only one is protected from this, as has been said. But in explaining to you this step in spiritual development, I have at the same time shown you how this development creates the possibility of a deeper penetration into material processes. This is the extraordinary thing. One who functions in the spirit simply as an abstractionist will be relatively powerless in the face of natural phenomena. One who really raises himself to the spirit is actually able to see more deeply into nature. He then grows together with other natural phenomena as he has already grown together with time and space.

We must now consider on the one hand all the things we have just tried to look at and on the other hand those things that we have encountered in looking at heat phenomena. What have we encountered in these heat phenomena? We followed the rise in temperature as we warmed a solid body to the melting point. We showed how the temperature rise disappeared for a time and then reappeared until the body began to boil, to evaporate. When we extended our observations, another fact appeared. We could see that the gas produced spilled over in all directions into its surroundings (see drawing, left), seeking to distribute itself in all directions, and could only be made to take on form if its own pressure were opposed by an equal and opposite pressure

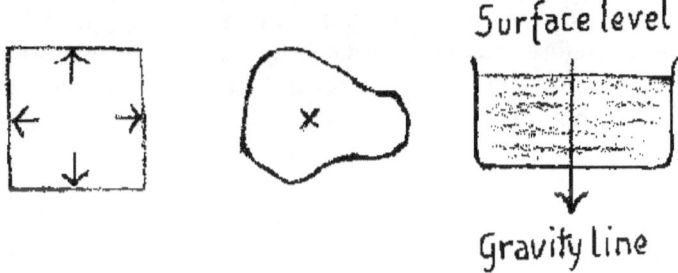

brought to bear from the outside. These things have been demonstrated by experiment and will be clarified further by other experiments. The moment the temperature is lowered to the point where the body can solidify, it can give itself form (see drawing, center). When we experience simply rise and fall of temperature, we experience what externally corresponds to "giving shape to," establishing a structure. We are experiencing the dissolution of form and the reestablishment of it. In the gaseous state form (structure) is dissolved, the solid state brings form (structure) into being.. We experience the transition between these two, and we experience it in an extremely interesting way. Imagine the solid and the gas and standing between them the liquid, the fluid body. This liquid need not be enclosed by a vessel surrounding it completely, but only on the bottom and sides. On the upper side, the liquid forms its own surface perpendicular to the line between itself and the center of the earth. Thus we can say that we have here a transitional state between the gas and the solid (see drawing, right). In a gas we never have such a surface. In a liquid such as water, there is formed a single surface. In the case of a solid, there is all around the body that which occurs in the liquid only on the upper surface.

This is an extremely interesting and significant relationship, for it directs our attention to the fact that a solid body has over its entire surface something corresponding to the upper surface of a liquid; the solid, however, determines the establishment of the surface by virtue of its own nature. How does the water establish its surface level? It is at right angles to the line joining it to the center of the earth. The *whole earth* conditions the establishment of this surface. We can therefore say that, in the case of water, each point within it has the same relationship to the entire earth that the points in a solid have to something within the solid. The solid therefore encompasses something that in the case of water resides in the water's relationship to the earth. The gas goes on strike, it diffuses. It does not enter a relationship to the earth at all. It totally eludes this relationship to the earth. Gases have no surface at all.

You will see from this that we are obliged to go back to an old conception. I called your attention in a previous lecture to the fact that the ancient Greek physicists called solid bodies "earth." They did not do this out of some superficial concept such as has been ascribed to them by people today, but they did it because they were conscious of the fact that the solid, by itself, takes care of something that in the case of water is taken care of by the earth as a whole. The solid takes into itself the role of the earthly. It is entirely justified to put the matter in this way: the earthly resides within a solid. In water it does not entirely reside within, but the whole earth takes up the role of forming a surface on the liquid.

You see, therefore, that when we proceed from solid bodies to water, we are obliged to extend our considerations not only to what actually lies before us; in order to get an intelligent idea of the nature of water, we must extend them to include the water of the whole earth and to think of this as a unity in relation to the central point of the earth. To observe a "fragment" of water as a physical entity is as absurd as to consider a cut-off fragment of my little finger as an organism. The fragment would die at once. It only has meaning as an organism if it is considered in its relation to the whole organism. Water does not in *itself* have the meaning that the solid has in itself. It has meaning only in relation to the whole earth. And so it is with all liquids on the earth.

And again, when we pass on from the fluid to the gaseous, we come to understand that the gaseous removes itself from the earthly domain. It does not form normal surfaces. It partakes of everything that is not terrestrial. In other words, we must not merely look on the earth for what is active in a gas; we must consider what surrounds the earth to help us out, we must go out into space and seek there the forces involved. When we wish to learn the laws of the gaseous state, we become involved in nothing less than astronomical considerations.

Thus you see how these things are related to the whole terrestrial scheme when we examine the phenomena that up to now we have simply gathered together. And when we come to a point such as the melting or boiling point, very significant things arise. For when we consider the melting point, we pass from the terrestrial condition of a solid body, in which it determines its own form and relations, to something that includes the whole earth. The earth begins to take the solid captive when the solid passes into the fluid state. From its own kingdom, the solid enters the terrestrial kingdom as a whole when we reach the melting point. It ceases to have individuality. And when we carry the fluid over into the gaseous condition, then we come to the point where the connection with the earth as shown by the formation of a liquid surface is loosened. The instant we go from a liquid to a gas, the body loosens itself from the earthly domain, as it were, and enters the realm of the extraterrestrial. We must consider the forces active in a gas as having escaped from the earth. When we study these phenomena, therefore, we cannot avoid passing from the ordinary physical-terrestrial into the cosmic. For we are no longer in contact with reality if our attention is not turned to what is actually working in the things themselves.

But now we encounter other phenomena. Consider a fact like the one with which you are very familiar and to which I have called your attention, namely that water behaves very unusually, that ice floats on water, or, stated otherwise, is less dense than water. When it passes into the fluid condition its temperature rises, and it contracts and becomes denser. Only by virtue of this fact can ice float on the surface of water. Between zero and four degrees, water shows an exception to the general rule that we find when temperature increases, namely that bodies become less and less dense as they are heated. This range of four degrees, in which water expands as the temperature is lowered, is very instructive. What do we learn from this range? We learn that the water begins to struggle. As ice it is a solid body with a solid's inner relationships, a kind of individuality. Now it is to pass over selflessly into relation to the whole earth, but it doesn't pass into this state of selflessness easily. It struggles against the transition to an entirely different sphere. It is necessary to consider such things, for then we begin to understand why, under certain conditions, the temperature rise as determined by a thermometer disappears, say at the melting or boiling points. It disappears just as our bodily reality disappears when we rise to the realm of imagination. We will go into this matter a little more deeply, and it will not appear so paradoxical when we try to clear up the following question: what happens when a heat condition obliges us to raise the temperature to the third power, which means in this case to go into the fourth dimension, thus passing out of space altogether? Let us place this proposition before our souls at this time, and tomorrow we will speak further about it. Just as it is possible for our bodily activity to pass over into the spiritual when we enter the imaginative realm, so we can find a path leading from the external and visible in the realm of heat to the phenomena lying behind that are indicated by our thermometer when the temperature rise we are measuring with it disappears before our eyes. What lies behind this disappearance? This is the question we are asking ourselves today. Tomorrow we will speak of it further.

Lecture VI

*Stuttgart,
March 6, 1920*

Today we will first examine a few phenomena in which heat, pressure, and the expansion of bodies are related. You will see that by observing several phenomena together we can experience how the path is opened to an understanding of what heat really is.

First we will turn our attention to what is revealed here in these three tubes. In the first one on the right, we have mercury in a barometer tube and on top of it is some water. Water placed in a space in such a way is continually evaporating. The water is in a vacuum, as we call it, in empty space, and we can say that the water is evaporating. The small amount of water in the tube evaporates continuously. We can determine that it is evaporating by the presence of water vapor in the space above the mercury. When you compare the height of the mercury column in this tube with the height here where the mercury is under the normal atmospheric pressure, and where there is no water vapor over the mercury, you will see that the level is lower in the tube containing water (see drawing, next page, *b* and 1). Naturally, the mercury column can only be lower than that in the barometer if there is a pressure on top of the column, for in the barometer tube there is no pressure on the top of the column. There is only empty space, so that the mercury column balances the atmospheric pressure and is equal to it. Here (1) it is forced down. When we measure, we find the value of this difference in height. And the amount of the depression is brought about by the pressure of the water vapor, by the vapor tension, as it is called. That is, the mercury column is forced down here (1).

We see, therefore, that vapor always presses on the confining walls. Moreover, a definite pressure corresponds to a definite temperature. We can demonstrate this by heating the upper part of the tube. You can see that when the temperature is raised, the mercury column sinks, due to the increased pressure of the vapor. Thus we see that the vapor increases its pressure on the wall more and more the higher its temperature. You can observe the mercury fall and can see how the vapor tension, the pressure, increases with the temperature. The volume occupied by the vapor is correspondingly increased.

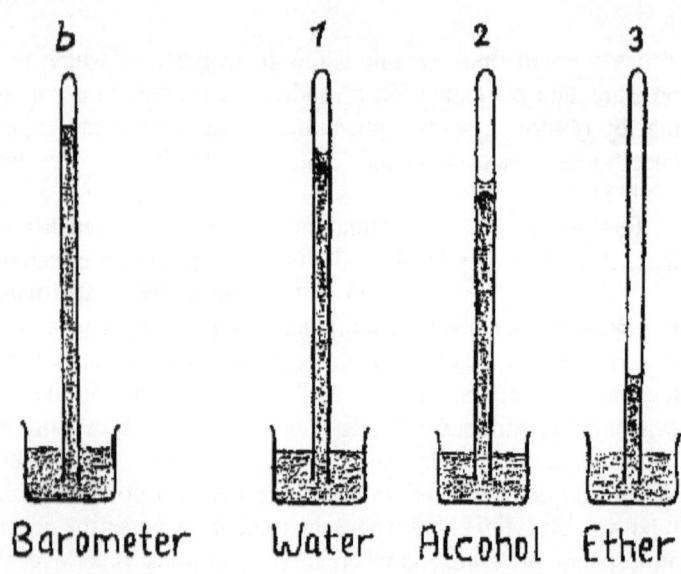

In the second tube (see drawing, 2) we have alcohol over the column of mercury. Again you can see the liquid alcohol occupying a definite space. It is also evaporating, and therefore this column too is less in height than the barometric column on the left. If I measure, I find that it is shorter than the column that is under the pressure of the water vapor. We must wait until the water vapor returns to the same temperature as it was before being heated. Then we will find that the vapor tension is also dependent on the substance we are using. The tension is greater in the case of alcohol than in the case of water. Here again, I can make the same experiment with heat. You will see that the pressure becomes considerably greater when we raise the temperature. When we cool the vapor to the same point at which it was at first, the mercury column rises, since with the smaller vapor tension there is less pressure.

Into the third tube (see drawing, 3) we have introduced ether under conditions similar to those in the other tubes. It is also evaporating. You see the column here is very low. From this you can see that ether evaporating under the same conditions as water shows an essentially different pressure. The pressure exerted by a gas is dependent not only on the temperature but on the material as well. Here too you can see the effect of increased temperature, shown by lowering of the column (tube heated slightly) due to the rise in vapor pressure, and you can see that the evaporated ether has a much stronger pressure. We will record the phenomenon in this case too, since we wish to come to our conclusion directly out of an overview of the phenomena.

Now there is a phenomenon that I would especially like to demonstrate to you. You know from the foregoing observations and also from elementary physics that solid bodies may be changed to liquids and liquids to solid bodies if we raise the temperature above the melting point and lower it below the melting point. When a fluid body is solidified by being brought below the melting point, it confronts us at first as a solid body. The remarkable thing, however, is that if we impose a stronger pressure on this solid body than that under which it solidified, it can again become liquid. Thus it can become liquid at a lower temperature than the one at which it solidified. You know that water changes to ice at 0°C.; thus it would have to be a solid body at all temperatures below 0°C. We will now carry out an experiment on this ice that will show you that we can make it a liquid without raising the temperature.

Ordinarily, we would have to raise the temperature to do this. In this case we will not raise the temperature but will simply exert a strong pressure on the ice. We can do this by hanging a weight over the ice by means of a thin wire.[21] The ice melts under the wire, and the wire cuts its way through the ice, because it liquefies under the pressure exerted by the wire. Now, you would expect this block of ice to fall apart into two pieces since it is being cut through the middle. If we could make it work faster, we could see the results of the experiment. (Note: the cutting of the block proceeded so slowly that the subsequent comments were added at the end of the lecture.) If you will now step up here and examine the block of ice, you will find there is no reason to fear that the two halves will crash down when the wire has cut through the ice, for the solid ice grows together at once above the cut. Therefore the wire goes through the block, the weight falls off, and the block remains whole. You can see in this that fluidity is brought about under the pressure of the wire, but as soon as the fluid is released from the spot where the pressure is exerted, it solidifies and the block of ice becomes whole again.

At the temperature of ice, the state of fluidity establishes itself only under increased pressure. Thus a solid can be melted at a temperature below its melting point, but the pressure must be maintained if it is to stay melted. As soon as the pressure is released it reverts to the solid state.

I wish to present a third thing to you that will furnish further support for our observations. To illustrate it we can take any suitable substances making an alloy, that is, mixing without forming a chemical compound – the principle holds good for all of them. In this tube we have lead. Lead is a substance that melts at 327°C., which is the temperature at which it passes from the solid condition to the liquid state. In another tube we have bismuth, which melts at 269°C., and here we have tin, melting at 232°C. Thus we have three bodies, all of which have melting points over 200°C. Now we will first melt these three, bringing them into the fluid condition in order to form an alloy. They will mix without combining chemically. (Note: the three metals were melted and poured together.)

Now, you would naturally reason as follows: since each of these metals has a melting point above 200°C., it would remain solid in boiling water, for water has a melting point of 0°C. and a boiling point of 100°C. Therefore these three metals could not melt in boiling water. Let us carry out the experiment of bringing the alloy, the mixture of the three, into water, just at the boiling point of 100°C. In this way we can see how it acts. We hold the thermometer here in the fluid metallic mixture and read a temperature of 175°C. This shows that although no single metal was fluid at this temperature, the alloy is still fluid. We can state the fact thus – when metals are mixed, the fact is brought out that the melting point of the mixture is lower than the melting point of any of its constituents.[22] Thus you can see how bodies mutually influence each other. From this particular fact we can derive an important principle for our view of the nature of heat phenomena.

Here we have the alloy still fluid in boiling water that is at 100°C., and now we let the water cool, observing the temperature meanwhile. The alloy finally solidifies. By measuring the temperature of the water at this point, we have the melting point of the alloy and can show that this melting point is lower than the melting point of any of the single metals. (This is 94°C.)

We have now added these phenomena to the others in order to have a broader basis for our overview. Let us continue by connecting these things with what we considered yesterday in regard to the distinction between the solid, fluid, and gaseous or vaporous states. You know that solid bodies such as most metals and other mineral bodies do not occur in an indefinite form but in very definite shapes that we call crystals. We can say that under ordinary circumstances as they exist on the earth, solids occur in very definite shapes or crystal forms. This naturally leads us to turn our attention to these forms and to try to puzzle out how these crystals originate. What forces lie at the foundation of crystal formation? In order to gain some insight into these matters, it will be necessary for us to consider how solid bodies behave that are on the surface of the earth but not connected directly with the mass of the earth.

You know that when we are holding a solid in our hand and let go of it, it falls to the earth. In physics this is usually explained as follows: the earth attracts solid bodies, exerts a force on them; under the influence of this force – the gravitational force – the body falls to the earth. When we have a fluid and cool it so that it solidifies, it may also form definite crystal formations. The question is now, what is the relationship between the force acting on all solids – gravitation – to those forces that must be present and active in a definite way so that the solid body can manifest in crystalline shapes? You might easily think that gravity as such, through whose agency a body falls to the earth (if we even want to speak of forces such as gravity), that this gravitational force had nothing to do with the building of crystal form. For gravity affects all crystal forms. No matter what outer form an object may have, it is subject to gravity. We find, when we have a number of solids in a row and take away the support, that they all fall to earth in parallel fines. This fall may be represented in somewhat the following way (see drawing).

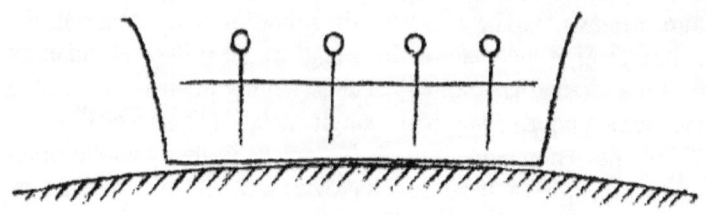

We can say that whatever form a solid may have, it falls along a line perpendicular to the surface of the earth. When now we draw the perpendicular to these parallel lines of fall, we obtain a surface parallel to the earth's surface. By drawing all possible perpendiculars to the lines of fall, we will obtain a complete surface parallel to the earth's surface. This is at first an imagined surface. We may now ask the question, where is this surface real? It is real in fluid bodies.[23] A liquid placed in a vessel shows as a real liquid surface that which I have assumed here as produced by drawing perpendiculars to the line of fall.

What is really involved here and what does it mean? What we have just put together is something of tremendous import. For imagine the following. Suppose someone were trying to explain the nature of the surface of the liquid and stated it in this way: every minute portion of the liquid has the tendency to fall to the earth. Since the forces of the liquid itself hinder this, the liquid surface is formed. It is the fluidity that causes the surface to form.

Picture to yourselves now the initial position of the solid bodies that you let fall, and then nature herself draws for you what you have drawn for purposes of this explanation. You must add the surface level in your thinking. I have said formerly that the surface level is to be thought of in its relation to solids as at right angles to their line of fall. When you think through these thoughts, you will make the curious discovery that what you normally do in order to bring thoughts in relationship to liquid is done for you by a number of solid bodies. They draw for you, as it were, what is present materially in the liquid. We may say that the body of a lower state of aggregation – the solid body in its behavior on the earth's surface – reveals to us as if in a picture what is actually present in the liquid, what is materially there in the liquid preventing the realization of this line as the drop line. This becomes pictorial if I consider the solid body in its entire relation to the earth.

Think what this enables us to do. When I draw the lines of fall and the surface formed under the impression of a system of falling bodies, then I have a picture of the gravitational activity. This is a direct image of liquid matter.

We can proceed further. When we leave water at any temperature sufficiently long, it dries up. Water is always evaporating. The conditions under which it forms a liquid surface are only relative. It must be confined all around except on the liquid surface. It evaporates continuously, and does so more rapidly in a vacuum. If we draw lines showing the direction in which the water is tending, their direction must indicate the movement of the water particles when it evaporates. When I actually draw these lines, however, I get nothing more or less than an image of a gas that is enclosed all around and is striving to escape in every direction (see drawing). There is a certain tendency on the surface of water which, when I picture it for explanatory purposes, represents a gas set free and spreading itself in all directions. We can state the proposition again in this way: what we observe in water as a force is actually a picture of what gas is as a material reality.

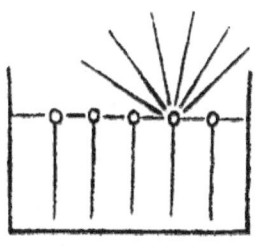
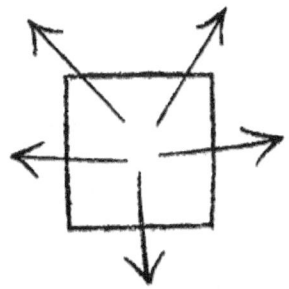

There is a curious fact brought out here. If we look at liquidity correctly from a certain point of view, we discover in this state a picture of the gaseous state of aggregation. If we properly observe solids, we perceive pictures of the fluid state of aggregation. In every subsequent state downward, pictures of the preceding state develop. Let us illustrate this by going from below up. We can say that in solids we discover the images of the fluid state, in the fluid we discover the images of the gaseous, in the gaseous we discover images of warmth. We will deal especially with this tomorrow. I will say only this today, that we have attempted to find the thought transition from gas to warmth. It will become clearer tomorrow.

Now when we have followed further this path of thinking, that:

- In solids we have the images of the fluid state;
- In fluids we have the images of the gaseous state;
- In the gaseous we have the images of the warmth state;

then we will have made an important step. We have advanced to the point where we have a picture in the gaseous state, which is accessible to human observation, of heat manifestations and even of the real nature of heat itself. We then gain the possibility, if we are seeking the images of heat in the gaseous state correctly, to explain the nature of heat even though we are obliged to admit that it is an unknown entity to us at the outset. We must look for images of the nature of heat in bodies in the gaseous condition.

But we must do this in the right way. When the various phenomena that we have described so far are handled as physics usually handles them, we get nowhere. If, however, we consider correctly the things that are revealed to us by bodies under the influence of heat and pressure, we will see how we actually come to stand before what the gases can reveal to us – the real nature of heat.

In cooling, the being of heat penetrates further into the liquid and solid states. We have to pursue the nature of this heat entity also in these states, although we can do it best in the gaseous condition where it is more evident. We must see whether in the fluid and solid states the nature of heat undergoes a special change within itself. Through this distinction between its manifestation in the gaseous realm, where it reveals itself to us in pictures, and its manifestation in fluids and solids, we must arrive at the real nature of heat itself.

Lecture VII

*Stuttgart,
March 7, 1920*

You will recall that yesterday we had a block of ice here that we would have expected to fall into two pieces as it was being cut by a wire from which a weight was hanging. Although you only saw the beginning of the experiment, you were able to be convinced that this was not the case, because as soon as the pressure of the wire liquefied the ice below, it immediately froze together again above the wire. That is to say, a liquefaction took place only in consequence of the pressure. Therefore, since we preserved the ice as ice, the warmth being is active here in such a way – I will use my expressions here very precisely – that the block joins itself together again.

Now this surprised you considerably at first, didn't it? But it surprised you only because you are not accustomed to the matter-of-fact observation necessary if you are really to follow physical phenomena. You are really making the same experiment all the time in another instance without wondering about it at all. For when you take up your pencil and pass it through the air, you are continually cutting the air and it is immediately closing up behind. You are then doing nothing other than what we did yesterday with the block of ice, but you are doing it in another sphere, in another realm. We can learn quite a lot from this observation, for we see that when we simply pass the pencil through the air (the conditions under which we do this will not be taken up now), the properties of the air itself bring about the closing up of the material behind the pencil. In the case of the ice we cannot avoid the thought that the warmth being enters into the process in such a way that it does the same as the air itself does when the pencil passes through. Here you have only a further extension of what I said to you yesterday. When you picture the air and imagine it cut by the pencil and closing up at once, the matter composing the air is responsible for all that you can perceive. When you are dealing with a solid body, such as ice, then warmth is active in the same way as the material air itself is in the other case.[24] That is, you meet here with a real picture of what goes on in warmth. And again you have confirmed that when we observe the gaseous or vaporous condition – air is vaporous, gaseous in reality – we have in the material process of the gases itself a picture of what takes place in the warmth being.

And if we observe warmth phenomena in a solid body, what we basically have is on the one hand the solid body and on the other hand that which proceeds in the realm of the warmth being. We see before our eyes, as it were, the phenomena within the realm of warmth that we also see taking place in the gas. From this we can conclude – or rather simply state, since it is only the obvious that we are presenting – that if we wish to approach the true being of warmth we must seek as well as we can to penetrate into the realm of the gaseous, into the gaseous bodies. And in what goes on in gases we will see images of what takes place within the warmth realm. By a manifestation of certain phenomena in gases, therefore, nature conjures up before our eyes, as it were, pictures of processes in the nature of heat. Notice now that we are being led very far from the modern method of observation as practiced in natural science generally, not merely physics. Let us ask ourselves where the modern method really leads us ultimately. I have here a work by Edward von Hartmann[25], in which he treats the field of modern physics from his point of view. Here is a man who has created for himself a broad horizon entirely out of the spirit of the times and who we may say is thus in a position to speak about physics as a philosopher. Now it is interesting to see how such a man deals with physics, speaking entirely in the modern spirit. He begins the very first chapter as follows: "Physics is the study of transformations and movements of energy and of its separation into factors and its resultants." Having said this, he must naturally add a further statement: "Physics is the study of the movements and transformations of energy (force) and of its resolution into factors and its resultants. The validity of this definition is not dependent on how we consider energy. It does not rest on our considering it as something final, ultimate, nor on our looking upon it as really a product of this or that view of the constitution of matter. It presupposes that all perception and sensation point back to energy, that energy can change place and form and that, in accordance with its concepts, it can be analyzed."

Now what does it mean when one speaks in such a way? It means that an attempt is made to define what confronts us physically in such a way that there is no necessity to enter into its real nature. One forms a definition which, by its very nature, makes it unnecessary to enter into the real nature of what is defined. A certain concept of energy is formed, and it is said: everything that meets us from without, physically, is only a transformation of this energy concept. That is to say, everything essential is thrown out of one's concepts, and then it is believed with certainty that, even if nothing else can be grasped, at least secure definitions are acquired. But this sort of thing has found its way into our physical concepts to a most unfortunate extent. So completely has it become a part of our view of the physical that it is almost impossible today for us to do experiments that will reveal reality to us. All the laboratories that we depend upon to do physical research are completely given over to working out the theoretical views of modern physics. We cannot easily use what we have in the way of tools in order to penetrate physically into the nature of things.

The cure for this situation is that first a certain number of people should become acquainted with the necessary methodical consequences of actually entering into the being of physical phenomena. This group out of itself will then have to find the experimental method, the appropriate laboratory setup, to make possible a gradual penetration into reality. We do not need merely to overhaul our conceptual view of the world, but we need research institutes working according to our way of thinking.[26] We cannot proceed as rapidly as we should in getting people to consider anthroposophy unless we are able to take them out of the rut in which modern thinking runs. Just as the physicist can now point to factories to show plainly, very plainly, that what he says is true, so we must show people by experiments that what we say about things is correct. Naturally, however, we must penetrate to real physical thinking before we can do this. And to think in real physical terms it is necessary that we bring ourselves into the state of mind indicated in these lectures, especially yesterday's lecture.

Is it not true that the modern physicist observes what happens, and when he observes it he at once makes every effort to strike out from the perceived phenomena everything he cannot reduce to calculation? Let us now make an experiment in order to see before us today something that we will build on in the course of subsequent lectures. We set up this paddle that can be turned in a liquid and arrange it so that the paddle rotated by means of this apparatus will transmit mechanical work. As a result of the fact that this mechanical work is transmitted to the water in which the paddle is immersed, we will have a considerable rise in the temperature of the water. We thus see in the most elementary experimental way what is called the transformation of mechanical work into heat, or thermal energy, as it is called. We have now a temperature of 16°C, and after a short time we will note the temperature again. (Later the rise in temperature was determined.)

Let us now return for a moment to what has already been said. We have tried to grasp the physical destiny of corporeality by carrying the corporeality through the melting and boiling points, that is, by making solid bodies fluid and fluid bodies gaseous. I will now speak of these things in simplified terms.

We have seen that the fundamental property of solid bodies is the possession of form. The solid body emancipates itself, so to speak, from what is active in creating the form of a liquid, active at least relatively if the liquid does not evaporate in the course of time. The solid body thus has its form somehow. Liquids must be enclosed in a vessel, and in order to form a liquid surface such as we find everywhere on the surface of a solid, they require the forces of the entire earth. We have indeed brought this before our souls. This requires us to make the following statement: when we consider the liquids of the whole earth in their totality, we are obliged to consider them as related to the *one* body of the earth in its totality. Only the solids emancipate themselves from this relationship to the earth, they take on an individuality, assume their own form. If we now take the method by which ordinary physics represents things and bring it to bear on what is called gravity, on what causes the formation of the liquid surface, then we must do it in the following way. If we are to stick to what is observable, we must in some way introduce into individualized solid bodies the thing that is essential in this horizontal liquid surface. In some way or other, we must conceive of what is active in the liquid surface, and which is thought of under the heading of gravity, as being within solids; they then individualize gravity in a certain way. Thus we see that solids take gravity up within themselves.

On the other hand, we see that at the moment of evaporation the formation of a liquid surface ceases. Gas does not form a surface. If we wish to give form to a gas, to limit the space it occupies, we must do so by placing it in a vessel closed on all sides. In passing from the liquid to the gas, we find that the surface formation ceases. We see dissipated this last remainder of the earth-induced tendency to surface formation as shown by the liquid. And we see also that all gases are grouped together in a unity, as illustrated by the fact that they all have the same coefficient of expansion; gases as a whole represent material emancipated from the earth.

Now place these thoughts vividly before you: you find that as human beings on the solid earth – therefore as a carbonaceous organism – you are among the phenomena produced by the solids of the earth. The phenomena produced by solids are ruled by gravity which, as stated, manifests itself everywhere. As earthly human beings you have solids around you that have in some way taken up gravity for their form-building. But consider the phenomena manifested by the solids in the case I spoke of yesterday, where you added in thought a surface to the system – in this phenomenon you have a kind of continuum, something you can think of as a sort of invisible fluidity spread out everywhere. Thus the solids of the earth, in so far as they are free to move, represent a fluid in the sum of their manifestations. They constitute something similar to what is manifested in a material fluidity. We can therefore say: since we are placed on the solid earth, we perceive what is surface-forming in water and call it gravity.

Imagine now that as human beings we were able to live on a fluid cosmic body, being organized in such a way that we could exist on such a body; then we would have to live above the surface level of this liquid, and we would have the same relationship to the gaseous, striving outward in all directions, that we now have to the fluid. This means nothing more or less than that we would not perceive gravity. To speak of gravity would cease to have a meaning. Gravity is thus perceived only by those beings that live on a solid planet, and only those bodies are subject to it that are solid. Beings who could live on a fluid planet would know nothing of gravity. It would not be possible to speak of such a thing. And beings who lived on a gaseous planetary body would regard as normal something that would be the opposite of gravity, a striving in all directions away from the center. If I may express myself somewhat paradoxically, I might say that beings dwelling on a gaseous planet instead of seeing bodies falling toward the planet would see them always flying off. If we are really to find the way here, we must think in really physical terms and not merely in mathematical terms. Then we can state the matter thus: gravity begins when we find ourselves on a solid planet. In passing from the solid to the gaseous planet, we go through a kind of null-point and come to an opposite condition to that on the solid planet, to a manifestation of forces in space that may be considered negative in respect to gravity (see drawing). You see, therefore, that as we pass through the material states, we actually come to a null-point in spatiality, to a null-sphere in spatiality. For this reason we have to consider gravity as something quite relative.

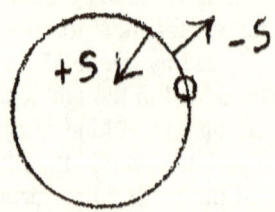

But when we conduct warmth to a gas (we did this experiment for you), this warmth that always raises the diffusing tendency in the gas shows you again the picture I am trying to bring before you. (See drawing, page 77) Is it not so that what is active in the gas really lies on the far side of this null-sphere to which gravity tends? Is it not possible for us to think the matter through further, still remaining in close contact with the actual phenomena, when we say that in going from a solid to a gaseous planet we pass through a null-point? Below we have gravity; above, for physical thinking, this gravity changes into its opposite, into a negative gravity. Indeed we find this, we do not simply have to think it. The being of warmth does the same thing that a negative gravity would do. Certainly, we have not completely attained our goal, but we have reached a point where we can comprehend the being of warmth in a relative fashion to the extent that the matter may be stated thus: the being of warmth manifests exactly like the negation of gravity, like negative gravity. When one therefore deals with physical formulae involving gravity and sets a negative sign in front of the symbol representing gravity, it is necessary to think of the magnitude in question not as a gravity quantity nor as a line of action of gravity but as a warmth quantity, a line of action of warmth. You can see that in this way we are able to suffuse mathematics with life. The formulae as they are given may be looked upon as representing a gravitational system, a purely mechanical system. If we set negative signs in front of the quantities, then we are obliged to consider as warmth that which formerly represented gravity. And you realize from this that we must grasp these things concretely if we are to arrive at real results. We see that in passing from the solid to the fluid we go through a condition in which form is dissolved. The form is lost. When I dissolve a crystal or melt it, it loses the form that it previously had. In passing into fluidity it takes on the form that is imposed upon it by virtue of the fact that it comes under the general influence of the earth. The earth gives it a liquid surface, and I must put this liquid into a vessel if I am to preserve it.

Now let us consider another general phenomenon that we will approach more concretely later. If a liquid is divided into sufficiently small particles, drops are formed that take on the spherical shape. Fluids have the possibility, when they are subdivided finely enough, of emancipating themselves from the general gravitational field and of manifesting in this special case what otherwise comes to light in solids as polyhedral form, as crystalline shape. In the case of fluids, however, the peculiarity is that they all take on the form of the sphere. If I now consider the spherical form, I may regard it as the synthesis of all polyhedral shapes, of all crystal forms.

When I now pass from the fluid to the gas, I have the diffusion, the dissolution of the spherical form, but in this case directed outward. And now we come to a rather difficult idea. Imagine to yourselves that you are observing some simple form, say a tetrahedron, and that you wished to turn it inside out as you might a glove. You will then realize that in going through this process of turning inside out it is necessary to pass through the sphere, and then the negative body appears, for which all relations are negative. As the tetrahedron is put through this transformation, you must imagine this negative body in such a way

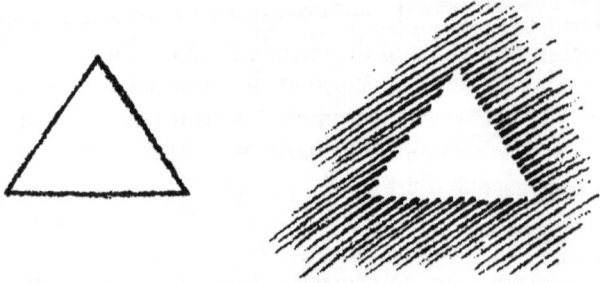

that the entire space outside the tetrahedron is filled; there it is gaseous. Within this filled outside space you must imagine a tetrahedral hole. There it is hollow. You must then make the quantities related to the tetrahedron negative. Then you have formed the negative, the opened-up tetrahedron, in place of the one normally filled with matter. But the intermediate condition between the positive and the negative tetrahedron is the sphere.[27] Every polyhedric body goes over into its negative only by passing through the sphere like through a null-point, a null-sphere.

Now let us follow this concretely in the case of actual bodies. You have the solid bodies with definite forms. They go through the fluid form, that is the sphere, and become a gas. If we wish to look rightly on the gas we must look upon it as form, but as negative form. We reach a type of form here that we can comprehend only by passing through the null-sphere into the negative. That is to say, when we go over to the gaseous – the picture of the phenomena of warmth – we do not enter into the region of the formless, we only enter a region more difficult to comprehend than the one in which we live ordinarily, where form is positive and not negative. But here we see that any body in which the fluid state comes into consideration is in an intermediate condition. It is in the state between the formed and what we call the "formless," or that of negative form.

Do we have any example where we can actually follow this, aside from what is in our immediate environment, an example we observe but do not actually experience? We can do this if we consider the phenomenon of the melting of a solid or the evaporation of a liquid. But can we somehow accompany this with our experience? Yes, we can, and as a matter of fact we do so continually. We experience this process by virtue of our status as earthly human beings, and because the earth, or at least the part of it on which we live, is a solid upon which there are other solids involving many phenomena that we observe. In addition, embedded within the earthly and belonging to it, there is the fluid state. The gaseous also belongs to it. Now there comes about a great distinction between what I will call *Wärmenacht* and *Wärmetag* (warmth night and warmth day). I use these terms in order to lead us nearer to an understanding of the problem. What is *Wärmenacht*? *Wärmenacht* is, in contrast to the *Lichtnacht* (light night), that which happens to our earth under the influence of the warmth being of the cosmos. And what happens? Let us consider these phenomena of the earth so that we can really see what can easily be understood by our thinking. Under the influence of the *Wärmenacht* the entire earth – we could limit ourselves at first by saying, the earth atmosphere – strives toward form. During the *Wärmenacht*, that is during the time when, with our earth being, we are not exposed to the sun being, when the earth being is left to itself and can emancipate itself from the influences of the cosmic sun being, the earth strives for form as the droplet takes on form when it can with-draw itself from the general force of gravitation. When we consider the continual striving of the earth for form, therefore, we have to do with the *Wärmenacht* rather than the *Lichtnacht*. But it is not said quite correctly if I say that the earth strives toward the droplet form. Rather, in the *Wärmenacht* the earth strives much more toward formation, toward crystallization. And what we experience every night is a continuous emergence of lines of forces striving toward crystallization, whereas during the day, under the influence of the being of the sun, there is a continual dissolving of this striving toward crystallization, a continual will to overcome form.

And we may then speak of the dawn and twilight of this warmth condition (*Wärmemorgendämmerung and Wärmeabenddämmerung*). By warmth dawn we mean that, after the earth has sought to crystallize during the *Wärmenacht*, this crystallization process dissolves again, and the earth goes through the spherical form in the warmth dawn, with its atmosphere; then it attempts to disperse itself. Following the *Wärmetag* comes a warmth twilight, in which the earth seeks again to form a sphere and to crystallize during the night. We thus have to imagine the earth as caught up in a cosmic process consisting of an attempt to draw together in the *Wärmenacht*, in which, if this were to proceed unhindered and the sun could be made to disappear, the earth could become a crystal. At the proper moment this is prevented when the earth is again led through the warmth dawn condition, through the spherical form. Then the earth seeks to dissipate itself into the cosmos until the warmth twilight again reestablishes the opposite forces. In the case of the earth, therefore, we do not have to do with something fixed in cosmic space but with something that continually vacillates in the cosmos between two conditions, *Wärmetag* and *Wärmenacht*.

You see, it is with things such as this that our research institute should concern itself. In addition to our ordinary thermometers, hygrometers, etc., we have to discover other instruments through which we could show that certain processes within the earth, especially within the fluid and gaseous portions, take place differently at night than during the day.

You can see that we are led here to a factual, physical way of observing by which we can finally demonstrate with appropriate instruments the delicate differences in all the processes in liquids and gases during the day and during the night. In the future we must be able to do a given experiment during the day and repeat it at a corresponding hour of the night, and we must have sensitive measuring instruments that will show us the difference in the way the process goes by day and by night. For by day those forces striving toward crystallization in the earth do not play through the process, but by night they do. Forces arise that come from the cosmos in the night. And these cosmic forces that seek to crystallize the earth must be revealed in the phenomena. This opens a way of experimentation that will show once again the relationship of the earth to the cosmos.

The research institutes that must be established in the future according to our anthroposophically oriented views of the world will have significant tasks. They must reckon with the things that today are taken into account only rarely. Of course we do take them into account today with light phenomena, at least in certain cases, for example when we have to darken the room artificially to evoke an artificial night, etc. But in other phenomena that take place within a certain null sphere, we do not. Instead, we arrive at the idea of displacing what we would discover as observable results within the bodies, and then talk of all kinds of forces that proceed between atoms and molecules.

The whole matter is based on our belief that we can now investigate everything during the day. We will discover differences, however, in crystallization depending on whether we carry out the same experiment during the day or during the night. This is the sort of thing our attention must be tuned to especially. And only on such a path will we come to a true physics. For today, physical phenomena really stand in a chaotic relationship to one another. We speak, for instance, of mechanical energy, of acoustical energy. But when we investigate these things physically it is not correctly considered that mechanical energies can proceed only where there are solid bodies in one way or another. Acoustical energies, however, always point to the fact that we are not in the sphere of the solid body anymore, so that then the fluid realm lies between purely mechanical and acoustical energy.

Indeed, when we leave the region in which we observe acoustical energy most readily, the gaseous region, then we come to the region of the next state of aggregation, to warmth. This lies above the gaseous, just as the fluid lies above the solid. We may tabulate these things as follows:

x
Warmth
Gaseous – Acoustical
Fluid
Solid – Mechanical.

We find the mechanical as a characteristic of the solid state. In the gaseous we find acoustical energy as the characteristic. Just as we have left out the fluid here, so we must leave out the warmth realm, and above we find something that I will indicate at this time by x. Thus we have to look beyond the warmth region for something. Between this x and our acoustic phenomena playing themselves out in the air would lie the being of warmth, just as the fluid condition lies between the gaseous and the solid states. We are trying, you see, to grasp the being of warmth in all the ways we can, to approach it by all possible paths. And when you say to yourselves that the fluid lies between the gaseous and the solid, and therefore the heat condition lies between the gaseous and x, you must in a similar way seek to pass from the warmth condition to the x condition. You must find something that lies similarly on the far side of the warmth being just as, for instance, the tone world as it is expressed in the air lies on this side of the warmth being.

By this means you see how to attempt to build real concepts of the physical that will lead you out of the merely abstract. Geometry can truly take hold of spatial forms, but mechanical concepts can never take hold of anything but the movement of solid bodies; in a way similar to geometry, these concepts we are now forming really take hold of physical being. They immerse themselves in the nature of the physical, and it is toward such concepts we must strive. Therefore I believe that this sort of exploration should belong to what lies at the foundation of the "Free Waldorf School."[28] We should attempt to extend the experimental in the way indicated here today. What is very much neglected in our study of physical processes – time and the passage of time – will thus be drawn into physical experiments.

Lecture VIII

Stuttgart,
March 8, 1920

Yesterday we carried out an experiment that brought to your attention the fact that mechanical work exerted by friction of a rotating paddle in a mass of water was changed into heat. You were shown that the water in which the paddle turned became warmer.

Today we will do just the opposite. We showed yesterday that we must seek for some explanation for the heat's coming into existence upon the expenditure of work, an explanation that accords with the facts better than this thought of a simple transformation of work into heat. Now let us follow the reverse process. First we will generate steam (see drawing, next page)[29] using a flame, raising the pressure of the vapor and thus bringing about a mechanical effect by means of heat, in a way similar to that by which all steam engines are moved. Heat is turned into mechanical work through the pressure change. By letting the pressure come through from one side we raise the piston up, and by letting the vapor cool the pressure is diminished, the piston goes down again, and we have performed mechanical work, consisting in this up-and-down movement. We can see the condensation water that reappears during cooling and runs into this flask. After we have let the entire process take place, after the heat that we have produced here has transformed itself into work, let us determine whether this heat has been entirely transformed into the up-and-down movement of the piston or whether some of it has been lost.

The heat that is lost, that is not changed into work, must appear as such in the water. In case of a complete transformation the condensation water would not show any rise in temperature. If there is a rise in temperature, which we can determine by noting whether the thermometer shows a temperature above the ordinary, then this temperature rise comes from the heat we have supplied. In this case, we could not say that the heat has been

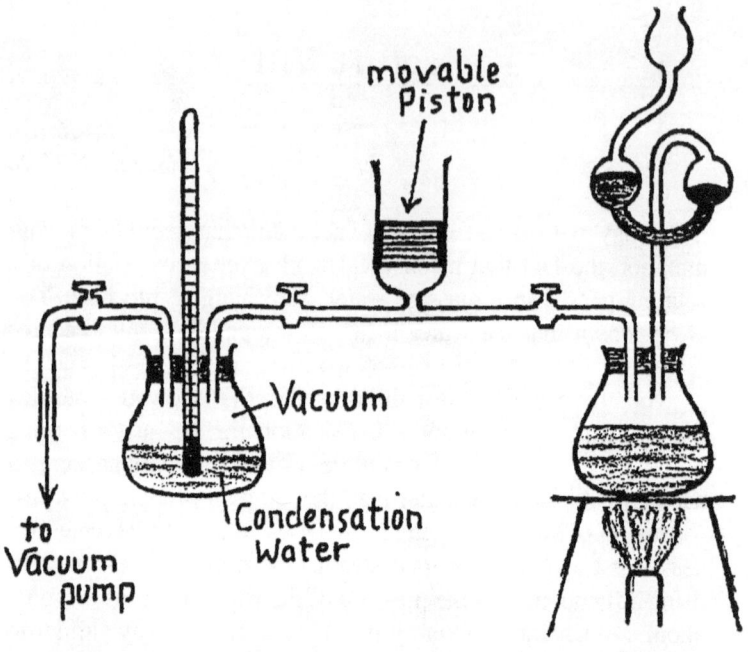

completely transformed into work; there would be a portion left over. Thus we can ascertain whether all of the heat has been transformed into work or whether some of it appears as heat in the condensate. The water is 20°C, and we can see whether the condensate is cooled to 20°C or shows a higher temperature, indicating a loss of heat to this condensate. Now we condense the vapor; the condensate water drops in the flask. A machine can be run in this way. If the experiment succeeds fully, you may determine for yourselves that the condensate shows a considerable increase in temperature. In this way we can demonstrate, when we carry out the reverse of yesterday's experiment, that it is not possible to get back all the heat that we have produced as mechanical work in the form of up-and-down movement of the piston. When heat is turned into work there is always some heat left over. The heat used in producing mechanical work does not change completely, but a portion always remains.

We wish first only to register this phenomenon, but now let us consider how ordinary physics and those who use its principles handle these things.

To begin with we have to deal with the fact that we do in fact change heat into mechanical work and work into heat, just as it is said we do. As previously stated, an extension of this idea has been made. It is supposed that every form of so-called energy – heat energy, mechanical energy, and the experiment may be made with other forms of energy – that all such energies can be transformed into one another. For the moment we will neglect the degree of the transformation and consider only the fact. Now, the modern physicist says that it is therefore impossible for energy to arise anywhere except from energy of another sort already present. If I have a closed system of energies, let us say of a certain form, and another energy appears, then this must be considered as transformation of the energies already present in the closed system. In a closed system, energy can never appear except as a transformation product. Eduard von Hartmann, who, as I have said, expressed current physical views in the form of philosophical concepts, states the so-called first law of the mechanical theory of heat as follows: "A perpetuum mobile of the first kind is impossible."

What is a perpetuum mobile of the first kind? It is a system in which energy would arise, as such, in a closed energy system. In this way Edward von Hartmann gathers together the series of phenomena we have considered and says "A perpetuum mobile of the first kind is impossible."

Now we come to the second series of phenomena illustrated for us by today's experiment. This is that in an apparently closed energy system, we have one form of energy changing into another form. In this transformation, however, it is apparent that a certain lawfulness underlies the process, and this is related to the quality of the energy. In the case of heat energy, the relation is such that it cannot change completely into mechanical energy, but there is always a certain amount unchanged. Thus it is impossible in a closed system to transform all the heat energy completely into mechanical energy. If this were possible the reverse transformation of mechanical energy completely into heat energy would also be possible. It would then be possible in a closed energy system for one type of energy to be transformed into another. This law is stated, again by Eduard von Hartmann, as follows: a closed energy system in which, for instance, the entire amount of heat could be changed into mechanical work, or where mechanical work could be completely changed into heat – when a cycle of complete transformation could exist – would be a perpetuum mobile of the second kind. But, says he, a perpetuum mobile of the second kind is impossible. Fundamentally, these are the principal laws of the mechanical theory of heat as this theory has been understood by thinkers in the realm of physics in the nineteenth century and the early part of the twentieth century.

"A perpetuum mobile of the first kind is impossible. A perpetuum mobile of the second kind is impossible." This matter is intimately connected with the history of physics in the nineteenth century. The first person to call attention to this apparent change of heat into other forms of energy or vice versa was Julius Robert Mayer.[30] He had observed, as a physician, that venous blood behaved differently in the tropics from the way it did in the colder regions, and from this he concluded that there was a different sort of physiological work involved in the human organism in the two cases. Using principally these experiences, he later presented a somewhat confused theory; this theory as he worked it out meant little more than this, that it was possible to transform one type of energy into another.

The matter was then taken up by various people, Helmholtz among others, and developed further. In the case of Helmholtz a characteristic form of physical-mechanical thinking was taken as the starting point for a consideration of these matters. If we consider the most important treatise by which Helmholtz sought to support the mechanical theory of heat in the 1840's, we see that ideas such as those expressed by Hartmann are really postulated as the foundation of the statement, "A perpetuum mobile of the first kind is impossible."[31] Since it is impossible, the various forms of energy must be transformations of each other. No form of energy can arise from nothing. The axiom from which we proceed – "a perpetuum mobile of the first kind is impossible" – can thus be changed into another: "The sum of the energy in the universe is constant. Energy is never created and never disappears; it is only transformed. The sum of the energy in the universe is constant."

These two principles fundamentally, then, mean precisely the same thing.

"There is no perpetuum mobile of the first kind."

"The sum of all the energy in the cosmos is constant."

Now, applying the method of thinking that we have used before in all our considerations, let us throw a little light on this whole point of view. When we do an experiment with the object of transforming heat into so-called work, some of the heat is lost during the transformation. Heat reappears as such, and only a portion of it can be turned into the other form of energy, the mechanical form. What we learn from this experiment we may apply to the cosmos. This is what the nineteenth century thinkers did. They reasoned somewhat as follows: "In the world around us mechanical work is present and heat is present. Processes are continually going on by which heat is transformed into mechanical work. We see that heat must be present if we are to be able to produce mechanical work. Just recollect how much our technical achievements rest on the fact that we cannot transform heat completely into mechanical work; a portion remains as heat. And since this is so, these remainders not capable of yielding mechanical work accumulate. These untransformed residues of heat accumulate, and the universe approaches a condition in which all mechanical work will have been turned into heat."

It has even been said that the universe in which we live is approaching what has been called by scholars its "warmth-death." We will speak in coming lectures of this so-called entropy concept. For the present our interest lies in the fact that, from an experiment, certain ideas have been drawn that bear on the fate of the universe in which we find ourselves.

Eduard von Hartmann has presented the matter very neatly. He says that physical observation shows that the world process in the midst of which we are living exhibits two sorts of processes: on the one hand, heat processes and on the other hand, mechanical processes. In the end, however, all mechanical processes will be transformed into heat processes. Then no more mechanical work will be able to be produced, and the universe will have to come to an end. Eduard von Hartmann thus says that physical phenomena show that the world process is running down. This is the way he expresses himself about the conditions within which we are living: we live in a universe whose processes preserve us but which has a tendency to become more and more sluggish and finally to lapse into a state of complete inaction. I am merely repeating Eduard von Hartmann's own words.

We must be clear about the following point. Is it ever really possible to call forth a series of processes in a closed system? Note well what I am saying. If I consider the totality of my experimental implements, I myself am certainly not in a vacuum, in empty space. And even if I believe myself to be standing in empty space, I still cannot be entirely certain whether this empty space appears empty only because I am unable to perceive what is really in it. *Do I therefore ever really carry out my experiments in a closed system?* Is it not so that what I carry out in the simplest experiment has to be thought of as enmeshed in the world process immediately around me? Can I conceive of the matter otherwise than in this way, that when I do all these things it is similar in relation to the whole world process to my taking a small needle and pricking myself here? When I prick myself here I experience pain that prevents me from having an idea that I would otherwise have had. It is quite certain indeed that I cannot consider merely the prick of the needle and the reaction of the skin and muscles as the whole of the process. In such a case I would not be looking at the whole process. The process is not entirely contained in these factors. Imagine for a moment that I am clumsy enough to pick up a needle, prick myself, and experience the pain. I would pull the needle away. What appears thus as an effect is in no way fully comprehended if I consider only what goes on in the skin. Drawing back the needle is in reality nothing other than a continuation of the first part of the process that I described. If I wish to describe the whole process, I must take into account that I haven't stuck the needle into my clothes but into my organism. This organism must be considered as a regulating whole, calling forth the consequences of the needle prick.

May I then speak of an experiment such as the one we have just seen in the following way: "I have produced heat and produced mechanical work. The heat not transformed remains in the condensation water as heat." In this statement, also, just as with the needle prick, I am not standing in relation to the whole matter. The production or retention of heat, its appearance in the condensation water, are related to the reaction of the whole great system, just as the reaction of my whole organism is related to the small activity of being pricked with the needle. What must be taken into account especially is that it is never valid for me to consider an experimental procedure as a closed system. I must keep in mind that this whole experimental procedure falls under the influence of the environment and of energies that work out of this environment.

 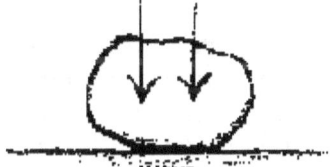

Consider along with this another fact. Suppose to begin with you have a vessel containing a liquid with its liquid surface, which implies an action of forces at right angles to this surface. Suppose now that through cooling, this liquid passes over into a formed solid. It is impossible for you to think of the matter otherwise than that the forces in the liquid are shot through by another set of forces. For the liquid forces make it imperative for me to hold this liquid, say water, in a vessel. The only form assumed by the water on its own account is the upper surface. When by solidification a definite enclosed form arises, it is absolutely necessary to assume that forces are added to those formerly present. Direct observation convinces us of this. And it is quite absurd to think that the forces creating the form are present in some way or other in the water itself. For if they were, there they would create the form in the water. They are thus added to the system, but they must have come into it from the outside. If we simply take the phenomenon as it is, we are obliged to say that when a form appears, it arises, in fact, as a new creation. If we simply consider what we can determine from observation, we have to think of the form as a new creation. It is simply a matter of observation that we bring about the solid state from the fluid. We see that the form arises as a new creation. And this form disappears when we change the solid back into a liquid. This is simply based on what is given as an observable fact. What follows now from this whole process, when one transforms the observable into a concept? It follows that the solid seeks to make itself into an independent unit, that it tends to build a closed system, that it enters into a struggle with its surroundings in order to become a closed system.

I might put the matter in this way, that here in the solidification of a liquid we can actually lay our hands on nature's attempt to attain a perpetuum mobile. But the perpetuum mobile does not arise, because the system is not left to itself but is worked upon by its whole environment. This observation can therefore be taken further: in space as given us, there is always the tendency at the various points for a perpetuum mobile to arise. But a counter tendency appears at once. We can therefore say that wherever the tendency arises to form a perpetuum mobile, the opposite tendency arises in the environment to prevent this. If you orient your thinking in this way you will see that you have thoroughly altered the abstract method of thinking of modern nineteenth century physics. The latter starts from the proposition that a perpetuum mobile is impossible, therefore etc., etc. If one stands by the facts, the matter must be stated thus: a perpetuum mobile is always striving to arise, and only the constitution of the cosmos prevents it.

And the form of the solid, what is it? It is the expression of the struggle. This picture that forms itself in the solid is the expression of the struggle between the substance as individuality, which strives to form a perpetuum mobile, and the hindrance to its formation by the great whole, the relative whole, in which the perpetuum mobile seeks to arise. The form of a body is the result of opposition to this striving to form a perpetuum mobile. It might be better understood in some quarters if, instead of perpetuum mobile, I spoke of a self-contained unit, a monad, carrying its own forces within itself and its own form-creating power.

Thus we arrive at a point where we have to reverse completely the entire starting point, not simply of nineteenth century physics but of the whole physical way of thinking of the nineteenth century. We do not have to modify physics itself, in so far as it rests on experiments dealing with facts. The physical way of thinking works with concepts that are not valid, and it cannot see that nature strives universally for what this thinking holds to be impossible. For this manner of thinking it is quite easy to explain the perpetuum mobile as impossible, but it is not impossible because of the abstract reasons advanced by the physicists. It is impossible because the instant the perpetuum mobile strives to establish itself in any given body, the environment becomes jealous – if I may borrow an expression from the realm of morals – and does not let the perpetuum mobile arise. It is impossible because of facts and not because of logic. You can appreciate how twisted a theory is that departs from reality in establishing its fundamental postulates. If reality is adhered to, it is not possible to get around what I presented to you yesterday in a preliminary, schematic way. We will elaborate that scheme in the next few days.

I said to you that we have, to begin with, the realm of solids. Solids are the bodies that manifest in definite forms. We have, touching on the realm of the solids, as it were, the realm of fluids. Form is dissolved, disappears, when solids become liquids. In the gaseous bodies we have a striving in all directions, a complete formlessness – negative form. Now how does this negative form manifest itself? If we look in an unbiased way on gaseous or aeriform bodies we can see in them what may be considered as corresponding to the entity elsewhere manifested as form. Yesterday I called your attention to the realm of acoustics, the tone world. In the gaseous state, as you know, the manifestation of tone arises through condensations and rarefactions. But when we change the temperature we also have to do with condensation and rarefaction in the body of the gas as a whole. Thus if we pass over the liquid state and seek to find in the gas what corresponds to form in the solid, we must look for it in condensation and rarefaction. In the solid we have a definite form; in the gas, condensation and rarefaction.

And now we pass to the realm adjacent to the gaseous. Just as the fluid realm borders on the solid, and just as we know how the solid pictures the fluid and the fluid pictures the gaseous realm, so the gas pictures the realm we must conceive as lying next to the gaseous, i.e., the realm of heat. The realm lying next above heat we will have to postulate for the time being, calling it the x region.

x		Becoming material – Becoming spiritual
Heat		
Gas	Negative Form	Condensation – Rarefaction
Fluids		
Solids	Form	

If now I seek to advance further, at first merely through analogy, I must look in this x region for something corresponding to but beyond condensation and rarefaction (this will be verified in our subsequent considerations); I must look for something like condensation and rarefaction there in the x region, passing over heat just as we passed over the fluid state below. If you begin with a solid, closed form, then imagine it to become gaseous and by this process simply to have changed its original form into another fluid form manifesting as rarefaction and condensation; if you then think of the condensation and rarefaction as heightened in degree, what is the result? As long as condensation and rarefaction are present, obviously matter is still there. But now, if you rarefy further and further you finally pass entirely out of the realm of the material. And this extension we have spoken of must, if we are to be consistent, be expressed in this way: a becoming material – a becoming spiritual. When you pass over the heat realm into the x realm, you enter a region where you are obliged to speak of the condition in a certain way. Holding in mind this passage from solid to fluid and the condensation and rarefaction in gases, you pass to a region of materiality and nonmateriality. You cannot do other than to speak of the region of materiality and nonmateriality. This means that when we pass through the heat realm we actually enter a realm that is in a sense a consistent extension of what we have observed in the realms beneath it. Solids oppose heat – heat cannot come to complete expression in them. Fluids are more susceptible to the intentions of heat. Gas completely follows the intention of heat. In gases there is a thorough manifestation of heat – it plays through them without hindrance, doing with the gas what it wants. In its material processes, gas is a picture of heat. I can state it thus: the gas is in its material behavior essentially similar to the heat entity. The degree of similarity between matter and heat becomes greater and greater as I pass from solids through fluids to gases. This means that liquefaction and evaporation of matter signify a becoming similar of this matter to heat. Passage through the heat realm, however, where matter becomes, so to speak, identical to heat, leads to a condition where matter itself ceases to be. Heat thus stands between two strongly contrasted regions, essentially different from each other: the spiritual realm and the material realm. Between these two stands the realm of heat. This transition zone is really somewhat difficult for us. We have on the one hand to climb to a region where things appear more and more spiritualized, and on the other hand to descend into what appears more and more material. Infinite extension upward appears on the one hand and infinite extension downward on the other (indicated by the arrows).

Now, the following analogy suggests itself; I'm setting it down before you because, through a direct pursuit of individual (or separate) scientific facts, a sound science may be developed. Also it is perhaps useful to contemplate these facts in the following way. If you observe the usual spectrum, you see the color sequence: red, orange, yellow, green, blue, indigo, violet.

Infra-red   r   o   g   gr   b   i   v   ultra-violet

⟵——————————————————————⟶

You have a band of colors following each other in a series of approximately seven nuances. But you also know that the spectrum does not break off at each end. If we follow it further beyond the red we come to a region where there is more and more heat, and finally we arrive at a region where there is no light but only heat, the infra-red region. On the other side of the spectrum, the violet, we also come to a region where we no longer have light. We come to the ultra-violet where only chemical action is manifested or, in other words, effects that manifest themselves in matter.

You also know, however, that according to the color theory of Goethe,[32] this series of colors can be bent into a circle and arranged in such a way that one sees not only the light from which the spectrum is formed but also the darkness from which it is formed. In this other spectrum the color in the middle is not green but the peach-blossom color, and the other colors proceed from this. When I observe darkness I obtain the negative spectrum. And if I place the spectra together, I have twelve colors that may be definitely arranged in a circle: red, orange, yellow, green, blue, indigo, violet; on this side the violet becomes ever more and more similar to the peach-blossom and there are two nuances between; on the other side there are two nuances between peach-blossom and red. You have in all, if I may use the expression, twelve color conditions. You can see from this that what is usually described as occurring with the linear spectrum can, by suitable means, also be brought about by this circle of

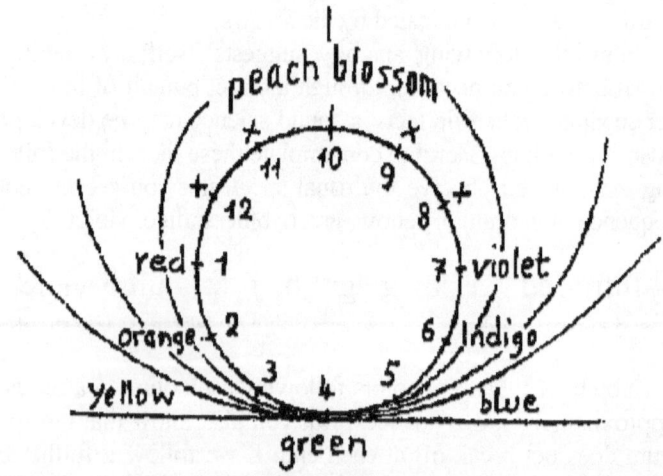

color: we can make it larger and larger, stretching out the five upper colors until they finally disappear. The lower arc becomes practically a straight line, and I obtain the ordinary spectrum of colors, having brought about the disappearance of the upper five colors.

So much for the colors. Could it not also be that here (see diagram, page 102) passing into infinity is somewhat similar to what I have done here to the spectrum? Suppose I ask what happens if what apparently goes off into infinity is made into a circle and returns on itself. Am I not perhaps dealing here with another kind of spectrum, one that on the one hand encompasses for me the conditions extending from heat to matter, but that on the other hand I can close up into a circle as I did in introducing peach-blossom into the color spectrum? We will consider this train of thought further tomorrow.

Lecture IX

*Stuttgart,
March 9, 1920*

The fact that we have spoken of the transformations of energy and force assumed by modern physics makes it necessary for us to turn our attention to the problem of indicating what really lies behind these transformations. We will approach this problem very systematically. To help in this, I wish to perform another experiment to be placed alongside yesterday's. In this experiment we will perform work through the use of a type of energy different from the one that is immediately evident in the work performed. We will, as it were, bring about in another sphere the same sort of picture that we evoked yesterday when we turned a wheel, put it in motion, and thus performed work. For the turning of the wheel can be applied in any machine, and the motion from this can then be utilized. We will bring about the turning of a wheel simply by pouring water on these paddles, and this water will bring the paddle wheel into motion by virtue of its weight. The force that exists in some way in the running water is transformed into the rotational force of the wheel.

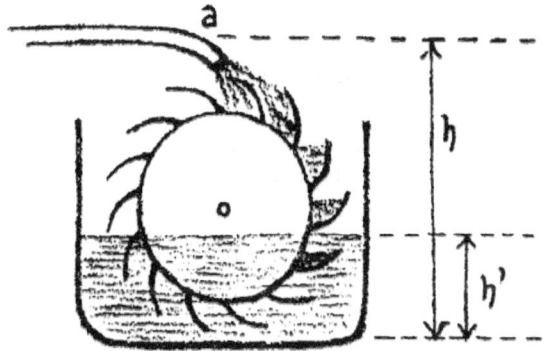

We will let the water flow into this trough in order to permit it to form a liquid surface as it did in previous experiments.

What we show is really this, that by forming a liquid surface below we make the motion of the wheel slower than it was before. It will slow down in proportion to the degree to which the lower level approaches the upper level. Thus we can say that if we indicate by h the total height of the water from point a here, where it flows onto the wheel (see drawing), and the perpendicular distance to the liquid surface by h', then we can state the difference as $h - h'$. We can further state that the work available for the wheel is connected in some way with the difference between the two levels. (In further considerations we will look into how this can be so.) In our experiment yesterday we also had a kind of difference in levels, $t - t'$. You will recollect that we denoted the heat of the surroundings at the beginning of our experiments by t', and the heat we produced in order to do work to raise and lower a piston we denoted by t. Therefore you can say that the energy available for work depends on the difference between t and t'. Here too we have something that can be designated as a difference in level.

I must ask you to note especially how both these experiments indicate that wherever we deal with what is called energy transformation, we have to take into account a difference in level. The part played by this difference in level that is really behind energy transformation – and that Eduard von Hartmann discarded before he even arrived at a definition of physical phenomena – we will find only if we pursue further yesterday's train of thought and bring it to a certain conclusion. To illuminate the whole scope of heat phenomena, we must emphasize again and again a beautiful remark of Goethe's regarding physical phenomena. He articulated this in various ways, somewhat as follows: "What of all outer physical apparatuses can compare to the ear of the musician, can compare with the revelation of nature that is given us in the musician's ear itself?"[33] What Goethe wished to emphasize by this is that we will never understand physical phenomena if we observe them separately from man himself. According to his view, the only way to understand physical phenomena is to study them in connection with the human being, to study the phenomena of sound, for instance, in connection with man's sense of hearing. But we have seen that great difficulties arise when we try in this way to bring the phenomena of heat in connection with the human being, when we really seek to connect heat with the being of man.

Even the facts that have led to the discovery of the modern, so-called mechanical theory of heat support this view. Indeed, what haunts this modern mechanical theory of heat had its origin in an observation of the human organism made by Julius Robert Mayer. Julius Robert Mayer, who was a physician, had noticed from taking blood samples in the tropical country of Java that the venous blood of tropical people was redder than that of people in northern climates. He concluded correctly from this that the process involved in the coloration of the blood varies depending on whether a person lives in a warmer or cooler climate, thus needing to give off less or more heat to his surroundings. This in turn involves a smaller or greater oxidation through breathing. Essentially he discovered that this inner work that man engages in, as it were, this absorption of oxygen, is intensified if it is less necessary for man to work with his outer environment. Thus the human being of the tropics, since he loses less heat to his environment, is not obliged to set up as active a relation to the outer oxygen as he would if he gave off more heat to his environment. In order to maintain his life processes and exist at all on the earth in the cooler regions, man is obliged to tie himself in more closely with his environment. In the colder regions where he works more intensely in connection with his environment, he must take in more oxygen from the air than in the warmer zones, where he labors more intensely in his inner nature.

Here you get an insight into the inner workings of the whole human organization. You see that it only needs to become warmer and the human being then works more in his inner individuality than he does when his environment is colder and he is thereby obliged to work more actively with his outer environment. From this presentation of a relationship of man to his environment proceeded the study that resulted in the mechanical theory of heat. These observations led Julius Robert Mayer in 1842 to submit his small paper on the subject to the *Poggendorffschen Annalen*.[34] From this paper arose the entire movement in physics that we know about. This is interesting, since the paper that Mayer submitted to the *Poggendorffschen Annalen* was returned as entirely lacking in merit. Thus we have the odd circumstance that physicists today say that we have guided physics into entirely new channels; we think entirely differently about physical phenomena from the way they did before the year 1842. But attention has to be called to the fact that the physicists of that time, and they were the best physicists of that period, had considered Mayer's paper to be entirely without merit and would not publish it in the *Poggendorffschen Annalen*.[35]

In a certain sense it might be said that his paper brings to a conclusion the kind of view of the physical in relation to man that was expressed in Goethe's statement though not brought to fruition. After this paper, a physics arose that sees the salvation of physics in considering physical facts separately from the human being. This is indeed the principal characteristic of modern physics. Many publications proclaim this idea as necessary for the advancement of physics, stating that nothing must be introduced that comes from the human being himself, that has to do with his own organic processes. But in this way we shall arrive at nothing. We must therefore continue our train of thought of yesterday, a train of thought drawn from the world of facts and one that will lead us to bring physical phenomena nearer to the human being.

I wish to develop for you the essential thing once again. We proceed from the realm of solids and find a common property at first manifesting in form. We then pass through the intermediate state of the fluid, showing form only to the extent of making for itself a liquid surface. Then we reach the gaseous state where the property corresponding to form in the realm of solids manifests itself as condensation and rarefaction, even in a realm formless in nature. We then come to the region bordering on the gaseous, the heat region, which again, like the fluid, is an intermediate region; and finally we arrive at our x realm. Yesterday we saw that by pursuing our thought further we have to postulate in x processes of materialization and dematerialization. It is not difficult, then, to see that we can obviously go beyond x to a y and a z realm, just as in the light spectrum, for instance, we move from green to blue, from blue to violet, and then into ultra-violet.

And now it is a question of studying the mutual relations between these different regions. In each one we see appearing what

I might call definitely characteristic phenomena. In the lowest realm we see an enclosed form; in the gaseous realm we see a fluctuating form, so to speak, in condensation and rarefaction. This accompanies – and I am now speaking precisely – this accompanies the tone entity under certain conditions. When we pass through the warmth realm into the x realm, we see materialization and dematerialization. The question now arising is this: how does one realm work into another?

z	
y	
x	Materialization – Dematerialization
Heat region	
Gaseous bodies	Rarefaction – Condensation
Fluid bodies	
Solid bodies	Form
U	

I have already called your attention to the fact that when we speak of gas, the processes taking place in the gaseous realm present a kind of picture of what goes on in the realm of heat. We can say, therefore, that in the gas we find a picture of what goes on in the heat realm. We have to consider that gas and heat mutually interpenetrate each other so that gas in its material form does what the heat wishes; in the processes that take place within a gas-filled space we can see an image of warmth. The gas is taken hold of in its expansion in space by what the heat wishes. What is really taking place in the realm of heat expresses itself in the gas in the interpenetration of the two realms. Furthermore we can say that fluidity shows a relationship to the gaseous similar to that between the gaseous realm and heat. And solids show the same sort of relationship to fluids as fluids do to gases and gases do to heat.

What comes about, then, in the realm of solids? In this realm forms appear, definite forms, forms circumscribed within themselves. These circumscribed forms are pictures, as it were, of what is really active in fluids. Now we can pass here to a realm U, below the solid, whose existence we will at first merely postulate hypothetically; and let us try to create concepts in order then to see whether these concepts are somehow applicable in the realm of outwardly perceptible phenomena. By extending our thinking, which you can feel is rooted in reality, we can create concepts that we hope will then lead us, because they were gained from reality, a bit further into reality.

What must take place if there is to be such a reality as the U realm? In this realm there must be pictured what in solids is a manifested fact. In a way corresponding to the other realms, the U realm must give us a picture of the realm of solids. In the realm of solids, we have forms everywhere, everywhere forms that are formed out of their own inner being, or at least out of their relation to the world – we will consider this further in the next few days. Forms come into being, mutually interrelated.

Let us go back for a moment to the fluid state. There, through the outwardly enclosed surface level of the fluid, we have a body showing its relation to the entire earth. In gravity, therefore, we have to recognize a force akin to the creation of form in solids. In the U realm we must find something that happens similarly to the form-building in the world of solids, if we are to pursue our thinking in accordance with reality; this would parallel the picturing of the fluid world by solids. In other words, in the U realm we must be able to see an action that foreshadows the various formations of the solid world. We must in some way be able to see this activity. We must see how, under the influence of different forms related to each other, something else arises. Something must come into reality that arises under the influence of the varying forms in the solid world. Today we really have only the beginning of such an insight. Suppose you take a substance such as tourmaline, which carries in itself a principle of form. You then let this formed tourmaline act in such a way that form can act on form. I am referring to the inner formative tendency. You can do this by allowing light to shine through a pair of tourmaline crystals. At one time you can see through them, and then the field of vision darkens. You can bring this about simply by turning one crystal in relation to the other. You have thus brought their form-creating force into a different relationship. This phenomenon is inwardly related to the apparent passage of light through solid systems differing in form, showing us the so-called polarization figures. These polarization phenomena always appear when one form influences another. Here before our eyes we have the noteworthy fact that we look through the solid realm into another realm that is related to the solid, just as the solid is to the liquid. Let us ask ourselves now, how does it come about that, under the influence of the form-building force, something appears in the U realm that creates form in the realm of solids, just as gravity forms only the surface in the fluid realm? To this we must reply that this happens when we observe the so-called polarization figures that lie in a realm to be found beneath that of the solids. We are actually looking into a realm that underlies the world of solids.

But we see something else also. We might look for a long time into such a system of solids, and the different forces might be acting there upon each other in the most varied ways, but we would see nothing if there were not something else playing through these solids as the U realm permeates the world of solids. Light, for instance, penetrates in and makes this mutual interworking of the form-building forces visible for us.

What I have been describing here is treated by the physics of the nineteenth century in such a way that the light itself is said to give rise to the phenomenon, while in reality the light only makes the phenomenon visible. If one wishes to comprehend these polarization figures, one must seek for an entirely different source than the light itself. What is taking place has nothing to do with the light as such. The light simply penetrates this U realm and makes visible what is going on there, what is taking place there as a foreshadowing of the solid form. Thus we can say that we have to do with an interpenetration of different realms that we have simply unfurled here. In reality we are dealing with an interpenetration of different realms.

And now the facts lead us to the same point we reached in the realm of the gaseous, for instance, by means of the forces of form that arise at the same time in liquefied form. We will have better concepts of what has been said if we consider condensation and rarefaction in connection with the relationship of tone to the mediating organ of hearing. It is not necessary to identify entirely these condensations and rarefactions in a gaseous body with what we encounter as different effects of tone. We must rather look for something that appears in a corresponding way in the realm of gases through condensation and rarefaction. What really happens we must express as follows: what we designate as tone exists in an unmanifested condition. But when we bring about certain lawful condensations and rarefactions in the gaseous realm, then there occurs what we are conscious of in tone perception. Isn't this way of stating the matter entirely parallel to the following? We can imagine heat conditions in the universe where the temperature is very high – above 100°C. We can also imagine heat conditions where very low temperatures prevail. Between the two is a range in which human beings can maintain themselves. It is possible to say that in the universe wherever there is a swing from the condition of a very high temperature to a condition of a very low temperature, there is at some intermediate point a heat condition in which human beings could arise. The opportunity for the existence of the human being is there, if other necessary factors for human existence are present. But on no account would we say that man is the temperature swing from high to low and the reverse (for here the conditions would be right again for man's emergence). We would certainly never say that.

In physics, however, we are continually saying that tone is nothing but the condensation and rarefaction in the air; tone is the movement of waves expressed in the air's condensation and rarefaction. Thus we accustom ourselves to a way of thinking that prevents us from seeing the condensations and rarefactions simply as bearers of tone, and not constituting the tone itself. We should also imagine for the gaseous condition something that simply penetrates the gas but belongs to another realm; and this realm would provide the possibility, in the gaseous realm, of perceiving a mediation between it and our organs of hearing. Only concepts formed in this way about physical phenomena are really valid. If, however, one forms a concept in which tone or tone formations are merely identified with air vibrations, then one is naturally led to consider light also as merely ether vibrations. A person thus progresses from something that is inaccurately conceived to the creation of a world of thought-out fantasies resulting simply from inaccurate thinking. Many relationships spoken about by the physics particularly from the end of the nineteenth century are nothing but the creation of an inexact thinking. Following the usual ideas of physics, we bury ourselves in physical concepts that are merely the creation of inaccurate thinking.

But now we have to consider the fact that when we pass from the heat realm to the x, y, and z realms, we have to pass out into infinity, and here, from the U region, we must also step into the infinite.

Recollect now what I brought to your attention yesterday. When we try to get an idea of the spectrum as it ordinarily appears to us, we have to go from the green through the blue to the violet and then off to the infinite, or at least to the undetermined. The same is true at the red end of the spectrum. But we can imagine the spectrum in its completeness as a series of twelve independent colors that now array themselves in a circle, with

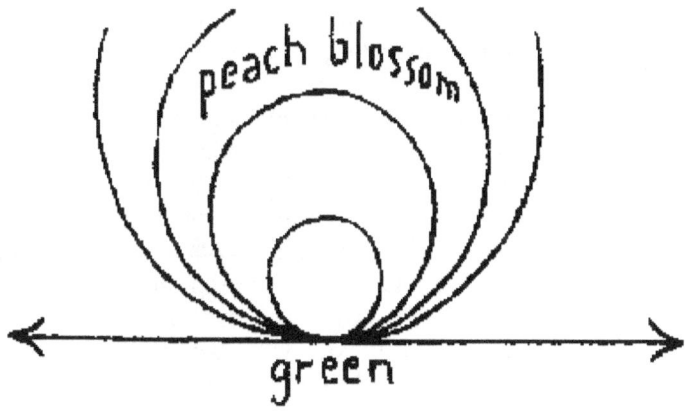

green below and peach-blossom above, and ranged between these the other colors. Then we can imagine that the circle becomes larger and larger; the peach-blossom disappears above, and the spectrum extends on one side beyond the red and on the other beyond the violet. In the ordinary spectrum, therefore, we really have only a part of what would be there if the entire color series could appear in the manifest world surrounding the human being. Only a portion is present.

Now here is a very remarkable thing. I believe that if you take the ordinary presentation of optics in the physics books and read what is given there as an explanation of a special spectral phenomenon, namely the rainbow, you will be uneasy if you are a person who likes clear concepts. For the explanation of the rainbow is given in such a way that one is left there without a bow. One is obliged to follow all sorts of things going on in the raindrop, and then it is necessary to put together this quite unified rainbow from the running together of extremely small reflections that are dependent on where one stands in relation to the rainbow. These reflections are said really to come from the raindrops. In brief, in this explanation you have an atomistic view of something that occurs in our environment as a unity.

But even more perplexing is the fact that this rainbow, and therefore the spectrum, conjured up before us by nature herself, never occurs singly. A second rainbow is always present, although sometimes not very obvious. Things that belong together cannot be separated. The two rainbows, of which one is clearer than the other, necessarily belong together, and if one is to explain this phenomenon, it is not possible to do so simply by explaining one strip of color. If we are to comprehend the total, or relatively total, phenomenon, we must make it clear to ourselves that something else is in the center and that it has two borders. One border is the clearer rainbow, and the other border is the more obscure bow. We are dealing with a picture that appears to us in the greatness of nature herself and which is, in fact, an integral portion of the entire universe. We must comprehend it as something unified. Now, when we observe carefully we will see that the second rainbow, the accessory bow, shows colors in reverse order from the first. It may actually be considered as a kind of mirror image of the first. It reflects, so to speak, the first and clearer rainbow.

As soon as we go from the partial phenomenon, as it appears in our environment, to a relatively more complete one – when we conceive of the whole earth in its relation to the cosmic system – we see an entirely different aspect. I wish at first only to point to this phenomenon here. We will go into it more completely in the course of our considerations. But I wish to say here that the appearance of the second rainbow converts the phenomenon into a closed system, so to speak. The system is only an open one as long as I limit my consideration to the spectrum that is apparent. The phenomenon of the rainbow really leads me to think of the matter thus, that when I produce a spectrum experimentally, I grasp nature only at one corner, and the opposite corner escapes me. Something has slipped into the unknown, and I really have to add to the seven-colored spectrum the accessory rainbow.

Now keep this phenomenon in mind, with the ideas that arise from it, and recollect the previous ideas of reality that we have brought out here (see diagram, page 111). We are trying to close up the band of color that stretches into the indefinite on both sides and bring the two together. If we now do a similar thing in this other area, what happens? We pass from solids to the U region and beyond, but as we do this we also come back from the other end of the series and the system becomes a closed one. But now, when the downward path and the upward one come together to make a closed system, what does that form? What happens then?

I will try to lead you to an understanding of this: suppose you really go in one direction in the sense indicated in our diagrams.[36] Let us say we go out from the sphere where, as we have explained in these lectures, gravity becomes negative. We have arrived, as it were, in one of the spheres. From this sphere, suppose we go downward, and imagine that on our way down we pass through the fluid and then the solid realms. Now, if we go

further, we must really come back from the other side – it is difficult to draw this. Since we come back from the other side, what belongs to this other side has to insert itself into the realm from which we have just passed. This means that in passing from the solid to the *U* region – if I want to represent the whole cycle – I must bend what is at the other end of the series around and thrust is in here. I can sketch it in this way (see drawing).[37] From

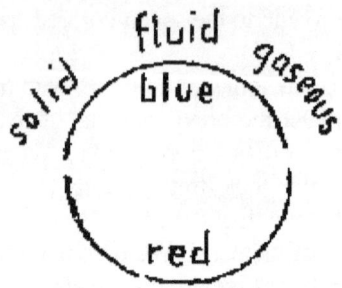

the Interpenetration of the world process

the null sphere I go through the fluid into the solid and then into the *U* region. Returning then, I come to the same point from the other side. Or, I might say, I observe the gas, which extends to here where I have colored with blue. But in the cosmic there comes from the other side that which inserts itself, interpenetrating, but appearing only as picture. It impregnates what comes back from the other side, so to speak, and manifests as picture. The fluid in its essence interpenetrates the sphere of the solid, running through that realm, where it appears as form. Similarly, something penetrates into the realm of gas, appearing there as tone, and we have indicated this toward the top of our diagram.

Turn over in your minds this returning and interpenetration in these world processes, and you will necessarily have to think not simply of a world cycle but of a certain sort of cycle. You will have to think of a world cycle that moves from one realm to another but in which any realm shows a reflection of other realms. In this way you get a basis for real thinking. This way of think

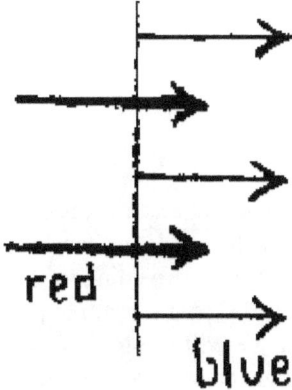

ing will help you, for instance, to see how light appears in matter, light that belongs to an entirely different realm; you will see that the matter has simply run away, while the light itself runs behind and slips into it. You will then, if you consider these things with mathematical formulae, have to extend your formulae somewhat.

You may consider these things as the ancient symbol of the snake that swallows its own tail, the symbol of ancient wisdom. The ancient wisdom represented everything symbolically, and we have to draw nearer to the reality itself.[38]

Lecture X

Stuttgart
March 10, 1920

Before we continue the observations of yesterday, which we have nearly brought to a conclusion, let us carry out a few experiments to give support to what we are going to say. First we will make a cylinder of light by allowing a beam to pass through this slit, and into this cylinder we will bring a sphere that is blackened with carbon so that light cannot pass through. We will indicate what happens by this thermometer (see drawing). You will

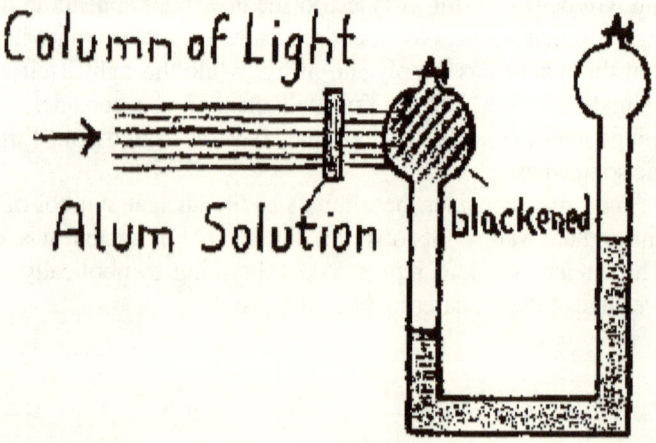

see that this cylinder of energy, which reveals itself outwardly as light passing into the sphere, reveals its effect by causing the mercury column to sink. Thus we are dealing with something that otherwise occurs under the influence of expansion. And indeed, in this case we have to assume also that heat passes into the sphere, causes an expansion, and this expansion makes itself evident by lowering the column of mercury. If we placed a prism in the path of the light we would get a spectrum. We do not form a spectrum in this experiment, but rather we catch the light – we gather it up and obtain a very marked expansion as a result of gathering up what is in this energy cylinder. You can see the mercury definitely dropping.

Now we will place an alum solution in the path of the energy cylinder and see what happens under the influence of this solution. You will see after a while that the mercury will come again to exactly the same level in the right- and left-hand columns of mercury. This shows that originally heat passed through, but under the influence of the alum solution the heat is blocked off and does not go through. The apparatus then comes only under the influence of the heat generally present in the space around it, and the mercury readjusts itself to equilibrium in the two tubes. The passage of heat is stopped as soon as I put this alum solution in the path of the energy cylinder. That is to say, from this cylinder which yields for me both light and heat, I separate out the heat and permit the light to pass through. Let us consider just this at first, although something else also still rays through. We can see that we are able to treat the spreading of the light-heat energy in such a way that we permit the light to pass on, and we separate out the heat by means of the alum solution.

This is one thing we must keep in mind at first simply as a phenomenon. There is another phenomenon to be brought to our attention before we proceed with our considerations. When we study the nature of heat, we can do so by heating a body at one particular spot. We then notice that the body gets warm not only at the spot where we are applying the heat but that one portion shares its heat with the next portion, then this with the next, etc., and that finally the heat is spread over the entire body. And this is not all.

If we now bring another body in contact with the warm body, the second body will become warmer than it formerly was. In modern physics this is ordinarily explained by saying that heat is spread by conduction. We speak of the conduction of heat. The heat is conducted from one portion of a body to another portion, and it is also conducted from one body to another in contact with the first. Already a very superficial observation will show you that this conduction of heat varies with different materials. If you grasp a metal rod in your fingers by one end and hold the other end in a flame, you will soon have to drop it, since the heat travels rapidly from one end of the rod to the other. Metals, it is said, are good conductors of heat. On the other hand, if you hold a wooden stick in the flame in the same way, you will not have to drop it quickly due to the conduction of heat. Wood is a poor conductor of heat. Thus we may speak of good and poor conductors of heat. Now this can be made clearer by another experiment. And unfortunately we are unable to make this experiment today. It has again been impossible to get ice in the form we need. At a more favorable time the experiment can be made with a lens made of ice as we would make a lens of glass. Then from a source of heat, a flame, this ice lens can be used to concentrate the heat rays just as light rays can be concentrated (to use ordinary terminology). A thermometer can then be used to demonstrate the ice lens' concentration of the heat passing through it (see drawing).

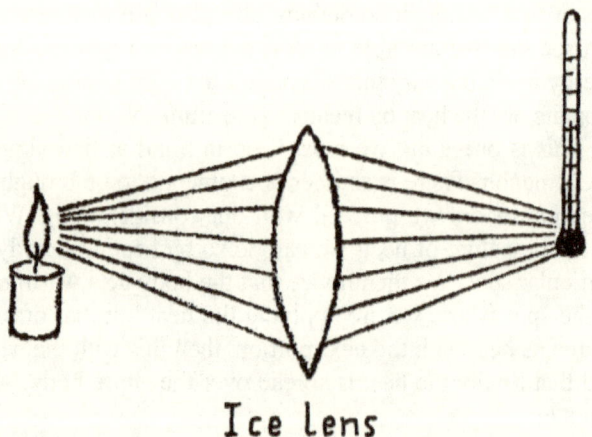

Ice Lens

Now you can see from this experiment that here there is a question of something very different from heat conduction, even though there is a transmission of the heat; otherwise the ice lens could not remain an ice lens. What we have to consider is that the heat spreads in two ways. In one form, the bodies through which it spreads are profoundly influenced, and in the other form it is a matter of indifference what stands in the heat's path. In this latter case we are dealing with the spreading of the real being of heat, with the spreading of heat itself. If we wish to speak accurately, we must ask what is actually spreading when we apply heat and see a body gradually getting warmer piece by piece; is it not perhaps a very confused statement of the matter when we say that the heat itself spreads from particle to particle through the body, since we are unable to determine anything about the process except the gradual heating of the body?

You see, I must emphasize to you again that we have to create very accurate ideas and concepts. Suppose, instead of simply perceiving the heat in the metal rod, you had a large iron rod, heated it here, and placed a row of boys on it. As it became hot the boys would cry out, first one, then the second, then the third, etc. One after another they would cry out. But it would never occur to you to say that what you heard from the first boy was conducted to the second, the third, the fourth, etc. When the physicist applies heat at one spot, however, and then perceives it further down the rod, he says that the heat is simply conducted. He is really observing how the body reacts, one part after another, giving him the sensation of warmth, just as the boys give a yell when they experience the heat. You cannot say, however, that the yells are transmitted.

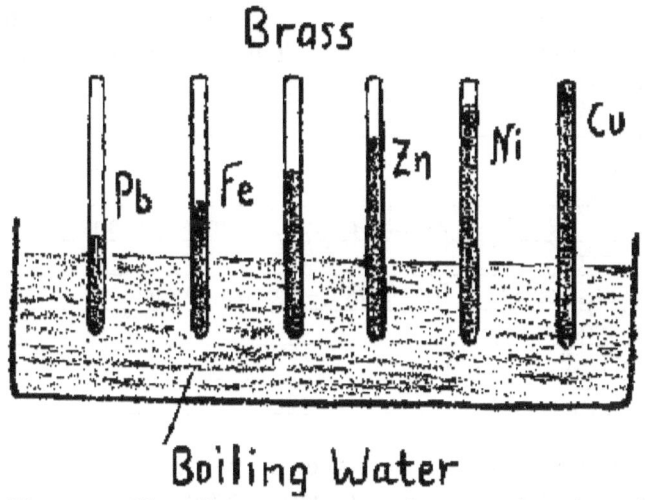

Now we will perform another experiment to show how different metals that we have here in the form of rods behave differently regarding what we are accustomed to calling the conduction of heat. We will strive now to get some really valid ideas about this. We have hot water in this vessel (see drawing). By placing the ends of the rods in the water, they are heated. Now we will see how this experiment comes out. One rod after the other will get warm, and we will have a kind of graduated scale before us. We will be able to see the gradual spreading of the effect of the heat in the different substances. The iodide of mercury on the rods, used to indicate rise in temperature, becomes red in the following order: copper, nickel, zinc, tin, iron, and lead. Among these metals, therefore, the lead is the poorest conductor of heat, as it is said.

I am showing you this experiment to help us form an overview of heat phenomena in order gradually to rise to an understanding of what the nature of heat is in its reality.

Now, from our remarks yesterday we have seen that when we turn our attention to the realm of corporeality, we can distinguish the realm of the solids by looking for that which shapes (forms or structures) itself. We then have the fluids as an intermediate state, and then we go over to the gaseous realm. In the gaseous we have, corresponding to form in the solid, condensation and rarefaction. Then again we have a kind of intermediate state, exactly as we would expect, namely, the heat condition. We have seen why we can place it as we do in the series (see diagram).[39]

z	
y	
x	Materialization – Dematerialization
Heat region	
Gaseous bodies	Rarefaction – Condensation
Fluid bodies	
Solid bodies	Form
U	

Then we come, as I have said, into an x region, where if we pursue this train of thought, we have to assume processes of materialization and dematerialization; then we would pass to a y realm and a z realm. This is all similar to the way in which in the light spectrum we find the transition from green through blue to violet and then apparently on to infinity. Yesterday we also determined that we have to continue below the solid realm into a *U* region. Thus we can picture the world of our corporeality as arranged in an order analogous to the spectrum. This is exactly what we picture if we wish to remain in the domain of reality.

Now let us extend the ideas of yesterday. In the case of the spectrum, we picture what disappears at the violet and red ends of the linear spectrum as bent around into a circle. In this different realm of the states of aggregation, we can picture in exactly the same way that the two ends of the series do not disappear into infinity. Instead, what apparently goes off into the indefinite on one side and what goes off into indefiniteness on the other may be considered as bending around, and then we have a circle before us, or at least a line whose two ends meet.

The question now arises, what is to be found at the point of juncture? When we observe the usual spectrum, at least, we can find something at this point. In Goethe's optics you know that if we consider the spectrum as a whole, with all its colors, it shows as its middle color green on one side, taking the bright spectrum. On the other side, when we make a dark spectrum, peach-blossom forms the middle color. Thus we have green, blue, and violet extending to peach-blossom on one side, and on the opposite side green, yellow, orange, and red extending to peach-blossom. By closing the circle we note that at the point where it closes, there is the peach-blossom color.

If we now construct a similar circle in our thinking for the various states of aggregation, what do we find at the point of juncture? This brings us to an enormously important point. What must we place in the spectrum of the states of aggregation that will correspond to the peach-blossom of the color spectrum? Perhaps it will be easier for you to grasp the idea that simply springs from the facts, if I had introduced it in the following way. What is it that we have before us, that disappears, as it were, in opposite directions – just as the color spectrum disappears beyond the red and the violet? What is it? It is nothing less than the whole of nature. The whole of nature is included in it. For in the whole of nature you cannot find anything not included in the form categories we have mentioned. Nature disappears from us on the one side when we go through the states of corporeality into heat and beyond. She disappears from us on the other when we follow form through the solid realm into the sub-solid where we saw the polarization figures, where form works on form. The tourmaline crystals show us now a bright field, now a dark one. Merely by the mutual effect of one form on another, dark and light fields appear alternately.

It is now essential for us to determine what we should place here, when we follow nature in one direction until we meet what can be characterized as streaming from the other side. What stands there? Nothing stands there but the human being as such. The human being is inserted at that point. Man, taking up what comes from both sides, is placed at that point. And how does he take up what comes from one side and from the other? From the side below (see diagram, page 124), he is formed. When we examine his form among other formed bodies, we are obliged to say that the human being also has a form. Thus the forces that give form elsewhere are also within man. And now we must ask ourselves, do these form-giving forces belong in the sphere of consciousness? No, they are not in human consciousness. Think of the matter for a moment. You cannot attain a real understanding of the human form from what you can see in either yourselves or other human beings. You cannot at first arrive at a concept of this form through inner experience. We are formed, but this form is not given in our immediate consciousness.

What do we have in our immediate consciousness in the place of form? This can be experienced only when one learns to observe the development of man's physical body gradually and in an unbiased way. When the human being first enters physical existence, he must be related very plastically to his formative forces. That is, he must form his body to a large extent. The nearer we approach the condition of childhood, the greater the forming activity in our own body, and as we grow older there is a withdrawal of the formative forces. In proportion to the withdrawal of our formative forces, the forces of our conscious mental activity appear. The more the formative forces withdraw, the more this other force advances. The more we lose the capacity to form ourselves, the more we can have ideas regarding form. This is simply an obvious truth. During the growth period of the human being, this can be noticed as an obvious fact, just as other clear facts can be noticed.

From this, however, we can say that we are able to experience formative forces. Forces that create form outside the body can be experienced. And how do we experience them? Through their becoming mental activity within us. Now we are at the point where we can bring the formative force to the human being. This formative force is not something that can simply be conjured up. Answers to the questions that nature poses us cannot be drawn from speculation or philosophizing but must be derived from reality. And in reality we see that the formative force reveals itself where form dissolves, as it were, into our mental activity, where it becomes mental activity. In our mental images we experience that which eludes us outwardly as force in the formation of our bodies.

If we place the human being here[40] then we can state the matter as follows: man experiences as ideas the forces of form welling up from below. What does he experience coming down from above? What does man experience beginning with the realms of gas and heat? Here again, when you look at the human being in an unprejudiced way, you have to ask yourselves: how does man's will relate itself to the phenomena of heat? You need only consider the matter physiologically to see that we need to go through a certain interaction with outer nature in order to produce warmth, in order to come to the will. Indeed heat must appear if willing is to become a reality. We have to consider will as akin to heat. Just as the formative forces of outer objects are akin to mental activity, so we have to consider everything manifested outwardly as heat as being related to what we find active in our will. Heat must therefore be looked upon as will, or we may say that we experience the being of heat in our will.

How can we define form when it approaches us from without? We see it, this form, in any given solid body. We know that if conditions are such that this form can be transformed by our life processes, mental images will arise. These mental images are not within the outer formation. It is somewhat as if I observed the soul-spiritual element separated from the body in death. When I see form in outer nature, what brings about the form is not there. It is truly not there. Just as the soul-spiritual element is not within a corpse but has been in it, so is that which determines form not within the object. If I therefore turn my eyes in an unprejudiced way toward outer nature, I have to say that something works in the process of form building – I will not say was active now, as *was* the case in the corpse, but rather is *becoming* active, so that we still see it – that lives in me as mental activity.

If I perceive heat in nature, I experience the same thing that is active in me in a certain way as will. In the thinking and willing human being, we have what meets us in outer nature as form and heat respectively.

But there are all possible intermediate stages between will and thought. A reasonable self-examination will soon show you that you never think without exerting your will. Exerting the will is particularly uncomfortable for modern man. He is more prone to allow the unconscious will to determine the course of his thoughts; he does not like to send will impulses into the realm of thought.

But entirely will-free thought content does not really exist, just as will not oriented by thought also does not exist. Thus when we speak of thought and will, of mental activity and will, we are dealing with extreme conditions, with what from one side builds itself as thought and from the other side builds itself as will. We can therefore say that in experiencing within ourselves will permeated by thinking and thinking permeated by will, we experience truly and essentially the outer forming activity and the outer nature of heat in nature. There is only one possibility for us here, and that is to seek in the human being for the essential being of what meets us in outer nature.

And now let us pursue these thoughts further. If you follow further the conditions of corporeality on the one side, you can say that you proceed along a line, as it were, into the indefinite. In the other direction you likewise proceed along a line into the indefinite. How must it be within the human being, however? Just the opposite must be the case here. Here again we must find what goes off into infinity. Instead of it going off into infinity so that we can no longer follow it, however, we must picture to ourselves that in the human being it disappears from space. What proceeds from below upward we must think of as disappearing from space. That is, the forces that are in heat must manifest themselves outwardly in their activity in man in such a way that they leave space. Likewise, the forces that produce form pass out of space when they enter the human being. In other words, in the human being we must come to a point where what appears spatially in the outer world as form and heat leaves space; where the impossibility arises that what becomes non-spatial can still be grasped mathematically.

I think we see here in an extremely significant way how a rational observation of natural phenomena obliges us to leave space the moment we approach the human being, provided we place him properly in the being of nature. We have to go to infinity above and below (see diagram, page 124). When we approach the human being, we must leave space. We cannot find a symbol that expresses spatially how the phenomena of nature meet each other in the human being. Nature properly conceived shows us that when we think of her in relation to the human being, we must leave her. Unless we do, when we consider the content of nature in relation to man we simply do not approach the human being.

But what does this mean mathematically? Suppose you set down the linear series along which you are following the states of aggregation to infinity. The values following one after another may be considered as positive. Then what works into the human being must be set down as negative. If you consider this series as positive, the effects in the human being have to be made negative. I think that what is meant by positive and negative will be cleared up by a lecture to be given by one of our members during the next few days. We have to conceive, however, of what we have seen here plainly – that the essential nature of heat, in so far as this belongs to the outer world, must be made negative when we follow it into the human being, and likewise the essential nature of form becomes negative when we follow it into the human being. Actually, then, what lives in the human being as mental image is related to form in the outer world as negative numbers are to positive numbers and vice versa, let us say, as credits and debits, though what is a credit here would be a debit there, and vice versa. What is form in the outside world lives in the human being as a negative. Thus if we say, "In the outside world there is some sort of a body of a material nature, "we have to add, "If I now think about its form, I must picture the matter in some way as negative." How is matter characterized by me as a human being? It is characterized by its pressure effects. If I go from the pressure effects of matter to my ideas about form, then the negative of pressure effects must come into the picture: suction. That is, we cannot conceive of man's ideas as material in their nature if we consider materiality as symbolized by pressure effects. We must think of them as the opposite. We must think of something active in the human being that is related to matter as negative is to positive. We must consider this as symbolized by suction if we think of matter as symbolized by pressure. If we go beyond matter we come to nothing, to empty space. But if we go further still, we come to less-than-nothing, to that which sucks up matter. We go from pressure to suction. Then we have that which manifests in us as mental activity.

And when on the other hand you observe the effects of heat, again you go over to the negative when it manifests in us. It moves out of space. It is, if I may extend the picture, sucked up by us. In us it appears as a counter image. This is how it manifests. Debits remain debits, although they are credits elsewhere. Even though our making external heat negative when it works within us results in reducing it to nothing, that does not alter the matter. Let me ask you again to note: we are obliged by force of the facts to conceive of the human being not entirely as a material entity; we must think of something in the human being that not only is not matter but is related to matter in all its effects just as suction is to pressure. Human nature properly conceived must be thought of as that which continually sucks up and destroys matter.

Modern physics has not developed at all this concept of negative matter, related to external matter as a suction is to a pressure. This is unfortunate for modern physics. What we must learn is that the instant we approach an effect manifest in the human being himself, all our formulae must be given another character. Will phenomena have to be given negative values in relation to heat phenomena; and thought phenomena have to be given negative values in relation to the form-giving forces.

Lecture XI

*Stuttgart,
March 11, 1920*

At this point I would like to build a bridge, as it were, between the deliberations in this course and those in the previous course.[41] Today we will study the light spectrum, as it is called, and its relation to the heat and chemical effects that come to us with the light. The simplest way for us to bring before our minds what we are to deal with is first to make a spectrum and learn what we can from the behavior of its various components. We will therefore make a spectrum by throwing light through this opening – you can see it here. (The room was darkened and the spectrum shown.) It can be seen on this screen. You can see that we have something hanging here in the red portion of the spectrum. We can observe something by means of this instrument. First we wish to show you how heat effects arise especially in the red portion of the spectrum. We can observe these effects through this expanding action of the energy cylinder on the air contained in the instrument, which expanding action in turn pushes the alcohol down on this side and up on this one. This depression of the alcohol column shows us that there is a considerable heat effect in this part of the spectrum.[42] It would also be interesting to show that when the spectrum is moved so as to bring the instrument into the blue-violet portion, the heat effect is not noticeable. This heat effect is essentially characteristic of the red portion.

And now, having shown the occurrence of heat effects in the red-yellow portion of the spectrum by means of the alcohol column, let us show the chemical activity of the blue-violet end. We do this by allowing the blue portion to fall on a substance that you can see is brought into a state of phosphorescence. From the previous course you know that this is a form of chemical activity. Thus you see an essential difference between the portion of the spectrum that disappears into the unknown on this side and the portion that disappears on this other side; you see how the substance glows under the influence of the chemical rays, as they are called.

Moreover, we could arrange matters in such a way that the middle portion of the spectrum, the real light portion, would be cut out. We could not do this with absolute precision, but we could make the middle portion approximately dark by simply placing in the light's path a solution of iodine in carbon disulfide. This solution has the property of stopping the light. It is possible to demonstrate the chemical effect on one side and the heat effect on the other side of this dark band. Unfortunately we cannot carry out this experiment completely but only mention it in passing. If I placed an alum solution in the path of the light, the heat effect would cease, and you would see that the alcohol column was no longer displaced because the alum, or the solution of alum, to speak precisely, would hinder the passage of the heat effect. Having placed alum in the light's path, you would soon see the column equalize, because the heat would no longer be present. We would have here a cold spectrum.

It is very interesting that a solution of aesculin placed in the path of the light source will cut out the chemical effect of the spectrum. Unfortunately we could not get this substance. The heat effect and the light effect would remain, but the chemical effect would cease.

Now let us place in the light's path the solution of iodine in carbon disulfide; the middle portion of the spectrum disappears. You see clearly the red portion – it would not be there if the experiment were an entire success – and the violet portion, but the middle portion is dark. We have succeeded partly in our attempt to eliminate the bright portion of the spectrum. By carrying out the experiment in a complete way, as certain investigators have done (for instance, Dreher,[43] fifty years ago), the two bright portions you see here can be done away with completely. Then the temperature-elevating effect may be demonstrated on the red side, and on the other side phosphorescence will show the presence of the chemically active rays. This has not yet been fully demonstrated, and it is of very great importance. It shows us how what we think of as active in the spectrum can be conceived in its general cosmic relations.

In the course that I gave here previously,[44] I showed how a powerful magnet works on the spectral relations. The force emanating from the magnet alters certain lines, changes the formation of the spectrum itself. It is only necessary for a person to extend the thought prompted by this in order to enter the physical processes in his thinking. You know from what we have already said that there is really a complete spectrum, a collection of all possible colors yielding a spectrum of twelve colors – we have a circular spectrum instead of the spectrum spread out in one dimension of space. In the circular spectrum we have green here, peach-blossom here, here violet, and here red, with the other shades between: twelve shades clearly distinguishable from one another (see drawing).

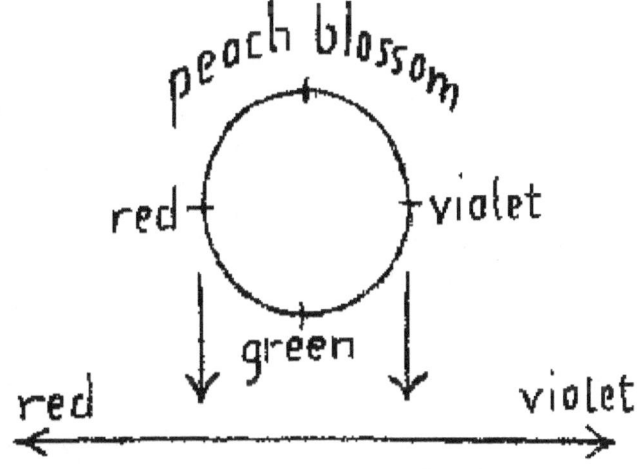

The fact is that under earthly conditions such a spectrum can be presented only as an image. When we are dealing with this spectrum in the domain of earthly life, we can do so only by means of a picture. The spectrum we actually get is the well-known linear one extending as a straight line from red through the green to the blue and violet – thus we obtain a spectrum formed from the circular one, as I have often said, by making the circle larger and larger, so that the peach-blossom disappears, violet shades off into infinity on one side, and red shades off on the other, with green in the middle.

We may ask the question: how does this partial spectrum, this fragmentary color band, arise from the complete series of color, the twelve-color series that must be possible? Imagine that you have the complete circular spectrum, and suppose forces act on it to make the circle larger and larger and finally to break it at this point (see drawing, previous page). Then, when the circle has broken, the action of these forces would make a straight line of the circle, a line extending apparently into infinity in each direction.

When we come upon this linear spectrum under our earthly conditions, we feel obliged to ask the question: how is this able to arise? It can arise only in this way, that the seven known colors are separated out. They are, as it were, cut out of the complete spectrum by the forces that work into it. But we have already come upon these forces in the earthly realm. We found them when we turned our attention to the forces of form. This too is a formative activity: the circular form is made over into the straight-line form. It is a form that we meet with here. And considering the fact that the inner structure of the spectrum is altered by magnetic forces, it becomes quite evident that the forces making our spectrum possible are everywhere active here. This being the case, we have to assume that our spectrum, which we consider a primary thing, has already working within it certain forces. Not only must we consider light variation in our ordinary spectrum, but we have to think of this ordinary spectrum as including forces that render it necessary to represent the spectrum by a straight line.

We must link up this line of thought with another, which comes to us when we go through the series – as we have done before frequently:

Materializing, dematerializing; dark, light	↓
Heat	
Rarefying, densifying	↑
Liquid	
Solid form	

from solid forms, through fluids, to condensation and rarefaction, i.e., gases, to heat, and then to that state we have called x, where we have materialization and dematerialization. Here we meet a higher enhancement of condensation and rarefaction, beyond the heat condition, just as condensation and rarefaction proper constitute an enhancement of forms becoming fluid. When form itself becomes fluid, when we have a changing form in a gaseous body, that is an enhancement of a definite form. And what occurs here? An enhancement of condensation and rarefaction. Keep this definitely in mind, that we enter a realm where we have an enhancement of condensation and rarefaction.

What do we mean by an "enhancement of rarefaction"? Well, matter itself informs us what happens to it when it becomes more and more rarefied, it tells us what matter is struggling with. When I make matter more and more dense, a light placed behind the matter no longer shines through. When matter becomes more and more rarefied, the light does pass through. When matter is rarefied enough, I finally come to a point where I obtain brightness as such. Therefore, what I bring into my understanding here in the material realm is empirically found to be the genesis of brightness. Dematerialization will appear to me as brightness; materialization will always appear to me as darkness. I thus have to think of brightness or luminosity as an enhancement of the condition of rarefaction; and darkening has to be thought of as a condensation, not yet intense enough to produce matter; but of such an intensity as to be just on the verge of becoming material.

Now you see how I can place the realm of light above the heat realm and how the heat realm is related to that of light in an entirely natural way. But when you recollect how a given realm always gives a sort of picture of the realm immediately above it, then you must look in the nature of heat for something that foreshadows, as it were, the conditions of luminosity and darkening. In the heat that appeared at one end of the spectrum, we must find something that provides a picture of a lightening and darkening. Keep in mind that we do not find only the upper condition in the lower, but also the lower condition is always in the upper. When I have a solid body, it can be altogether in the fluid realm with its solidity. What gives it form may extend over into the next realm, which is not characterized by form. If I wish to encompass reality with my concepts I must be clear that there is a mutual interpenetration of qualities of reality. This principle takes on a particular form, however, in the realm of heat; dematerialization works down into heat from above (see arrow, diagram page 134), while from the lower side the tendency to materialization works up into the heat realm.

Thus you see that I draw near to the nature of heat when I see in it on one side a striving for dematerialization and on the other a striving for materialization. If I wish to grasp the nature of heat, I can do it only by conceiving within it a life, a living weaving, manifesting itself everywhere as a tendency to materialization penetrated by a tendency to dematerialization. What an essential distinction exists between this conception of heat based on reality and the nature of heat as outlined by the so-called mechanical theory of heat of Clausius! In the Clausius theory we have atoms or molecules in a closed space, little spheres moving in all directions, colliding with each other and with the walls of the vessel in a purely external movement (see drawing). And it is positively stated that heat actually consists of

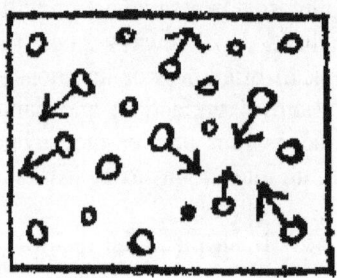

this chaotic movement, of this chaotic collision of material particles with each other and with the walls of the vessel. A great controversy arose as to whether the particles were elastic or nonelastic. This is of importance only as the phenomena can be better explained on the assumption of elasticity or on the assumption that the particles are hard, nonelastic bodies. This has given form to the conviction that heat is purely motion in space and so it is said: heat is motion.

Actually, we too must say that heat is motion, but in an entirely different sense. It is motion in which, wherever heat is manifested in space, there is a tendency to create material existence and to let material existence disappear again. It is no wonder that we also need heat in our organism. We need heat in our organism simply to change continuously the spatially extended into the spatially nonextended. If I simply walk through space, what my will is producing shapes the space. When I think about it, something completely outside of space is present. What makes it possible for me as a human organization to be inserted externally into the form relationships of the earth? When I walk over the earth, I change the entire earthly form. I change her form continually. What makes it possible that I am connected with everything on the earth and that I can form ideas outside of space, within myself, as observer of what is manifested in space? This is what makes it possible: my existence is enacted in the medium of heat and is thus continually enabled to transform material effects, that is spatial effects, into immaterial effects that no longer partake of the spatial nature. In myself I experience in fact what heat is in reality: intensive motion, motion that continually alternates between the realm of pressure effects and that of suction effects.

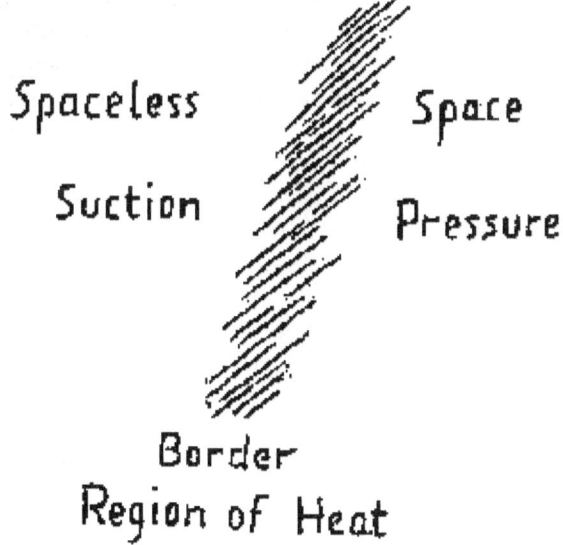

Assume that you have here (see drawing) the border between pressure and suction effects. The effects of pressure run their course in space, but the suction effects do not, as such, act in space – they operate outside space. For my thoughts, based on the effects of suction, take their course outside of space. Here on one side of this line (see figure), I have the nonspatial. And now when I conceive of what takes place neither in the realms of pressure or suction but on the border between the two, I am dealing with the things that take place in the realm of heat. I have a continual searching for equilibrium between pressure effects of a material sort and suction effects of a spiritual sort. It is quite remarkable that certain physicists have had these things right under their noses but refuse to consider them. Planck[45], the Berlin physicist, has made the following striking statement: if we wish to arrive at a concept of what is called ether nowadays, the first requisite is to follow the only path open to us, in view of the knowledge of modern physics, and consider the ether nonmaterial. This from the Berlin physicist, Planck. The ether, therefore, is not to be considered as a material substance.

But now, what we find beyond the heat region, the realm in which the effects of light take place, we consider so little allied to the material that we are assuming the pressure effects – characteristic of matter – to be completely absent, and only suction effects active there. This means that we leave the realm of ponderable matter and enter a realm naturally active everywhere but manifesting itself in a way diametrically opposed to the realm of the material. We must picture only suction effects active there, emanating from every point of space, while material things obviously manifest through pressure effects. Thus, indeed, we come to an immediate concept of the nature of heat as intensive motion, as an alternation between pressure and suction effects, but in such a way that we do not have, on the one hand, suction spatially manifested and, on the other hand, pressure spatially manifested. If we wish to comprehend the nature of heat, we must entirely leave the material world and with it three-dimensional space. If the physicist expresses certain effects by means of formulae, and he represents forces in these formulae, then in the case where these forces are expressed by a negative sign – when pressure forces are made negative – they become suction forces. Attention must be paid to the fact that in such a case one leaves space entirely. Consideration of such formulae leads us into the realm of heat and light effects. Heat effects are only half included, for in the realm of heat we have both pressure and suction effects playing into each other.

These facts, , can be given only theoretically today in this presentation in an auditorium. It must never be forgotten, however, that a large part of our technological achievement has arisen under the influence of materialistic concepts of the second half of the nineteenth century. Modern technology did not have ideas such as we are presenting, and therefore such ideas cannot arise in it. If you consider how fruitful the one-sided concepts have been for technology, you can imagine how many technical consequences might flow from adding to the modern technology – which takes into account only pressure forces – the possibility of making these suction forces fruitful also (and by these I mean not only spatially active suction, which is a manifestation of pressure, but suction forces qualitatively opposite to pressure forces).

Of course, much now incorporated in the body of knowledge known as physics will have to be discarded to make room for these ideas. For instance, the usual concept of energy must be thrown out. This concept rests on the following very crude notions: when I have heat I can change it into work, as we saw in the experiment from the up-and-down movement of the piston resulting from the transformation of heat. But we saw at the same time that the heat was only partly changed and that a portion remained, that only a portion was at our disposal to transform into what physics calls mechanical work, while the other portion could not be transformed in this way. This was the fact that led Eduard von Hartmann to enunciate the second most important law of modern physics: a perpetuum mobile of the second type is impossible.

Other physicists, Mach, for example, who is well known in connection with modern developments in this field, have done fundamental thinking on the subject.[46] Mach has thought along lines that show him to be a shrewd investigator but one who can only make use of his shrewdness under the influence of a purely materialistic view. Behind his concepts always stands the materialistic point of view. He shrewdly seeks to push forward and extend the concepts and ideas available to him. His noteworthy characteristic is that when he comes to the limit of the usual physical concepts, where doubts begin to arise, he writes the doubts down at once. This leads soon to despair, because he comes quickly to the limit where doubts appear, but his way of expressing the matter is extremely interesting. Consider how things stand when a man who has the whole of physics at his command is obliged to state his views as Mach states them. He says, "There is no sense in expressing as a work value a heat quantity that cannot be transformed into work." (We have seen that there is such a residue). "Thus it appears that the energy principle, like other understandings of substance, is valid only for a *limited* realm of facts. The existence of these limits is a matter about which we ordinarily are happy to deceive ourselves."

Consider a physicist who, upon thinking over the phenomena lying before him, is obliged to say that "There is in fact heat that I cannot turn into work. But there is no meaning in simply thinking of this heat as potential energy, as work that is simply not visible. I can perhaps speak of the transformation of heat into work within a certain realm, but beyond this realm it is no longer valid. Generally it is said that every energy is transformable into another, but this can be accepted only by virtue of a certain habit of thinking about which we gladly deceive ourselves."

It is extremely interesting to pin physics down at the very point where doubts are expressed, doubts that arise necessarily from a straightforward consideration of the facts. When physicists are obliged to make such confessions, does this not clearly reveal the way in which physics itself is overcome? For the energy principle is fundamentally nothing but a conjecture. One can no longer hold to the energy principle put forth as gospel by Helmholtz and his contemporaries. There are realms in which this energy principle can no longer be upheld.

Now let us ask the following: how can one make the attempt symbolically (for fundamentally it is symbolic when we try to sketch the outlines of something), how can we attempt to symbolize what occurs in the realm of heat? When you bring together all these ideas that I have developed here, and through which I have tried to reach the nature of heat in a real sense, you come to a concept of heat in the following way.

Picture to yourselves (see drawing) that here there is space (blue) filled with certain effects, pressure effects; here is the nonspatial (red) filled with suction effects. If you picture this now, you come here to a realm that is something different, that is always slipping in here and disappearing – we have projected out into space what can only be thought of as spatial/nonspatial, for the red portion must be thought of as nonspatial. You see the space here (blue and red) as a symbol of what is spatial/nonspatial. Think of something represented as "extensive" and "intensive," by which materiality continually arises. As substance appears, there enters in something from the other side that is immaterial, that slips into the substance and annihilates it; then we have a physical-spiritual vortex continually manifesting in such a way that what appears physically is annihilated by what appears as the spiritual. Therefore we have a vortex effect in which the physical comes into being that is then annihilated by the spiritual. We have a continuous interplay between the nonspatial and the spatial. We have a continual sucking up of what is in space by the entity that is outside space.

You must think of what I am describing to you here as shaped similarly to a vortex. But in this vortex you should see simply a visible extension of that which is "intensive" in its nature. In this way we approach, I might say figuratively, the nature of heat. We have yet to show how this nature of heat works so as to bring about such phenomena as conduction or the lowering of the melting point of an alloy below the melting point of its constituents, and what it really means that we should have heat effects at one end of the spectrum and chemical effects at the other.

We must seek the *deeds of heat* as Goethe sought out the *deeds of light*. Then we must see how knowledge of the nature of heat is related to the application of mathematics and how it affects the imponderables of physics. In other words, how are real mathematical formulae to be constructed that can be applied to heat and optics?

Lecture XII

*Stuttgart,
March 12, 1920*

The experiments we had anticipated carrying out today we will unfortunately have to postpone until tomorrow. At that time they will be arranged in order to show you what is necessary if I am to prove to you all that I wish to prove. Today, therefore, we will consider some things that, together with the experiments of tomorrow, will enable us to bring our considerations to a conclusion the following day.

To help reach an understanding of the nature of heat, I wish to call your attention to a certain fact. We must take this fact into account in developing our ideas on this subject: it is difficult to understand a transparent body. I am not speaking of heat now. When we have finished this exploration, however, you will see that we can get ideas helpful in understanding heat from the realm of light.

I said there is a certain difficulty in understanding what a relatively transparent body is and what an opaque body is, in other words, in understanding something as it reveals itself under the influence of light. I have to express this in a different way from what is ordinarily done. The customary way of describing the situation in physics would be as follows: an opaque body is one that by some peculiar property of its surface reflects the rays of light that fall on it and thus becomes a visible body. I cannot use this form of expression, because it is simply not a reflection of the facts; rather it is a statement of a preconceived theory and is not by any means to be taken as self-evident, for to speak of rays, of light rays, is theoretical. I have dealt with this already in my previous course on light. In reality everything we encounter is not light rays but an image, and we must hold this firmly in mind. As a matter of fact, we cannot simply say that a transparent body is one that by virtue of its inner molecular properties allows light to pass through, and an opaque body is one that throws the light back. For how can such a theory be substantiated? Recollect what I have said to you about the relationships of the various realms of reality: solids, fluids, gaseous bodies, x, y, z, and, bordering the solid below, the U region. If you keep this in mind, you will see that the light realm must have some kind of relationship to the realm of heat, and so also must the realm of chemical activity. On the other side, what we meet as the fluid form, so to speak, in heat or in gases must have some kind of relationship to the true essence of tone. For tones appear with the occurrence of condensation and rarefaction in gases or aeriform bodies.

We may therefore suspect that where we have assumed x, y, and z, we will find the essence of light. Now the question is whether we have to look in the same place that we have looked for the essence of light to find the nature of transparency of certain bodies. The nature of transparency is not necessarily able to be derived from that of light, nor from the relationship of light to solid bodies. We also have the U region, and this U region and its effects must have some kind of relationship to the solids on the surface of the earth. We must first at least ask the following question and then seek to apply the answer to this question to our consideration of these things: what influence does the U region have on solids, and, from the nature of this influence, can we derive anything that will show us the difference between transparent bodies and the ordinary opaque metals? Such questions must be considered first, and the way to answer them will appear if we now attempt to extend our ideas of yesterday regarding the nature of heat by adding certain other conceptions.

Heat phenomena, of course, are considered to belong to the realm of physics. Things such as heat conduction are included, thought of in the way I have described to you. This spreading of heat through conduction, and therefore through the heat condition's flow either through a body or from one body to another one touching it, has been observed. The flow of heat has been conceived of as though a kind of vague fluidity were involved. This may be compared to something readily observable in the outer world, namely the water in a brook that is at one point now and a moment later is at a distant point. It is pictured that heat flows from one point to another when the so-called conduction of heat takes place. This flow of the warmth condition has been considered by numerous people in this way; fairly lucid concepts are to be found in Fourier[47] (other investigators might also be cited), and to these we need only add a little to be able to see how these concepts will help establish the validity of the knowledge we have already gained here.

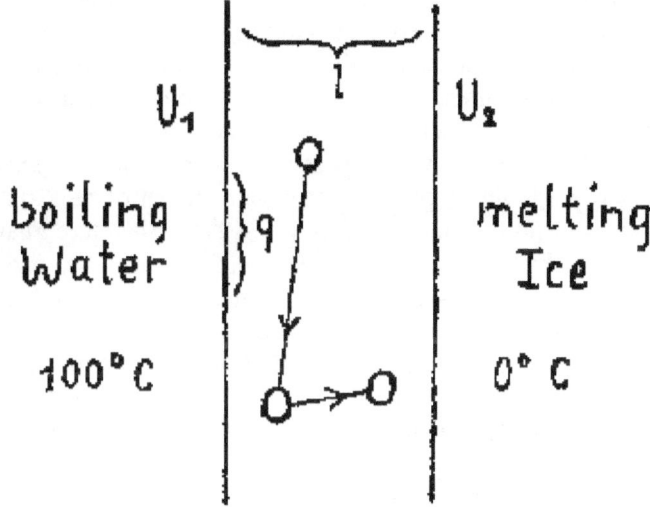

Imagine that we have an enclosed body of some kind of metal that is clearly delimited (see drawing) by a plane here and a plane here. Assume the planes to extend indefinitely upward and downward, and suppose them to consist of some sort of metal. Let us place boiling water in contact with the plane on one side, holding it at a temperature U_1, which in this case is 100°C. Next to the other plane we place melting ice to maintain it at a temperature U_2, which in this special case will be 0°C.

Considering the entire phenomenon, you will see that we have to do with a difference: here U_1, here U_2; $U_1 - U_2$ gives us the temperature difference. How the conduction of heat takes place depends on this difference in temperature. Obviously, the conduction of heat will proceed differently if the temperature difference is large than if it is small. To achieve the same effect, I need only a small quantity of heat if the temperature difference is small, whereas I need a large quantity of heat if the difference is great. Thus I must say that the quantity of heat needed to achieve a certain effect depends on this temperature difference, $U_1 - U_2$. Furthermore, it will depend not only on the difference,

U_1 - U_2 but on the thickness of the object, which I may denote by l (see drawing). The quantity of heat needed to achieve a definite effect is less if the thickness is great than if it is small. That is, the amount of heat needed is inversely proportional to l. I may calculate for a given cross section that I will call q how much heat I will need to achieve a certain degree of heat conduction. The larger the cross section, the greater the amount of heat required. Thus the amount of heat is directly proportional to q, and I must multiply by this factor.

Finally, the whole process is dependent upon time. A greater effect is produced by permitting a given amount of heat to act for a longer time, a smaller effect in less time. Therefore I have to multiply by the time factor, t.[48] Obviously, I must then multiply through by a constant representing the degree of heat itself, c, by something involving heat – since none of the quantities so far mentioned includes the heat – and thus I arrive at the necessary quantity of heat, w. This quantity of heat w is directly proportional to the temperature difference, U_1 - U_2, and to the other factors and inversely proportional to l. Now if you compare all the other factors with U_1 and U_2, you will see that in expressing what really flows we do not have to do directly with a heat quantity but with something related to heat, with a drop in temperature, with a difference in level. Always keep this in mind, please. Just as when we pour water through a sluice and turn a paddle wheel, and the motion is due to the energy arising from a difference in level, so here we have to do with a drop from one level to another, and it is this we must keep in mind.

Now we have to take up another consideration of Fourier's to draw nearer to the nature of heat. First we will work through these ordinary concepts, as it were, so as to move nearer to reality than the physicists of the nineteenth and twentieth centuries. So far I have taken into consideration only what happens when heat is conducted from one spot in the body to another, but I can assume that something goes on in the body itself. Let me now ask a question. Suppose we assume hypothetically that the progress of heat instead of being uniform from left to right was disproportionate within the body; how would we apply this formula to the inner lack of uniformity? If there is an irregularity in the distribution of heat, I must bring it into my considerations in some way. I must bring in the alterations in this difference in level that reveal themselves within, that is, my considerations must take into account what takes place in the body itself as the temperature effects equalize. As you can easily see, my formula can be transformed to reflect this. At first I have to say that:

$$w = \frac{U_1 - U_2}{l} \cdot t \cdot c \cdot q$$

Now I will no longer take into account the whole thickness of the object but will deal with small portions of it, and I will consider what happens in these small portions, as over the entire distance it is expressed by the factor $(U_1 - U_2) / l$. It is thus a question of dealing with minute distances within the body, which I represent by dx. I employ the differential ratio du/dx, where du represents an infinitesimal movement of heat. If this is considered for a small instant of time, I must multiply by dt, this being left out of account if I do not consider the time. Thus we have w as an expression of the quantity of heat transferred through a small distance in order to equalize the temperature within the body. The following formula expresses the effects of temperature fall within the body:

$$w = c \cdot q \frac{du}{dx} \cdot dt$$

In relation to this, I will ask you please to consider what we took up yesterday in a sketchy way and which will be clearer tomorrow when we have carried out the necessary experiments. Today, I will simply mention it since we must keep it in mind. I am referring now to the relationships between heat, light, and chemical effects in the spectrum. Yesterday I called your attention to the following fact: when we have an ordinary earthly spectrum (see diagram), in the middle are the actual light effects, toward one end the heat effects, and toward the other end the

← | Warmth | Light | chem. Effect | →

chemical effects.

Now we have to consider the following. We have seen that if we want to construct a picture of this spectrum we must not think of light, heat, and chemical effects as stretched out in a straight line. We go forward out of the plane here on the left to approach the appropriate symbol for heat, and toward the right backward out of the plane to approach the chemical effects (see

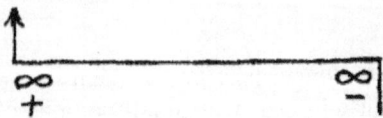

diagram). This could be reversed, but let us remain with it this way for now.

Thus it is not possible to remain in the plane of light effects if we wish to symbolize the heat effects; nor can we remain in this plane if we wish to symbolize the chemical effects. We have to move out of this plane. Now to visualize the whole matter, let us be clear how we are really to represent a heat quantity working within a body by means of our formula. How, then, must we represent quantitatively the relationship between it and the chemical quantity? We will not do this properly until we take into account the fact that we go one way to reach the heat and the opposite way to reach the chemical effects. This fact must be kept in mind if we are to orient ourselves. So if we consider w as a positive quantity here (we might also consider it negative), then we have to consider the corresponding diffusion of chemical effect as:

$$w = -c \cdot q \, \frac{du}{dx} \cdot dt$$

This equation corresponds to the chemical effect, and this one corresponds to the heat effect:

$$w = +c \cdot q \, \frac{du}{dx} \cdot dt$$

As a matter of fact, these things demonstrate for us an important point: that when we create formulae we cannot handle merely the mathematical quantities if we expect the formulae to express the relationships within a field of actual effects, an observed realm, where heat and chemical effects are manifesting themselves. In ordinary combustion, for instance, where we wish to bring heat and chemical effects into relation, we must, if we work with formulae, designate as positive what represents heat effects and as negative what represents the corresponding chemical effects.

Now if you carry your considerations further, you will see the following: if we think of heat as extending in one direction, so to speak, and chemical effects as extending in the opposite, then in the plane itself we have only what is actually present in light. But if you have reserved the positive sign for heat and the negative sign for chemical effects, you cannot use either of these for light effects. At this point you have to apply to the light effects a set of facts that today are only vaguely felt and not by any means explained, namely the relationship between positive and negative numbers and imaginary numbers. When you are dealing with light effects, you have to say:[49]

$$w = \sqrt{-1} \cdot c \cdot q \cdot \frac{du}{dx} \cdot dt$$

That is to say, if you wish to deal with the real relationships between heat, chemical, and light effects taking place in the same experimental field at the same time, you have to use imaginary numbers – your calculation has to involve the mathematical relations expressed in imaginary numbers.

We have already made the following statement[50], however: the spectral band that we can produce experimentally under earthly conditions is actually to be thought of as a circle that has been opened out. The complete spectrum would have the peach-blossom color above. If, by employing sufficiently great force you were able to bend the spectrum into a circle, you would bring together what apparently extends off into infinity on the left and on the right. Now, however, you can realize that this closing up cannot simply be thought of as being carried out in a circle in one plane. For as you go out through the heat region, you also go off forward to one side, and, proceeding through chemical effects, you go off backward to the other side. You are then apparently in the position of having to go into the infinite first on one side and then into the infinite on the other side. You have the awkward task of seeking an infinitely distant point first in one direction and then coming back from this infinitely distant point and entering the plane from the other side. This implies that the infinitely distant point on the left is the same as the one on the right: there, at least, you are in the same plane. Moreover, you are confused if you go in here, to the left and forward, and there, to the right and backward, unless you assume that to come back the infinity here and there must lead to the same point. You have to take a doubly complicated path. In order to discover the peach-blossom color, therefore, you must not only bend the spectrum in one plane but at right angles to this plane on each side.

If you imagine you are acting on the color band with, say, an electromagnet, you will have to turn the magnet to achieve this. That however makes you realize the following: that what you would then find couldn't be indicated by these (mathematical) symbols. One would have to use the *superimaginary numbers*,[51] which were presented to you yesterday during the discussion. You will perhaps recall that there is controversy about these superimaginary numbers. They are not readily handled mathematically and can have more than one meaning, so to speak. Some mathematicians even question whether there is any justification for them at all. Physics does not give us a definite formulation for the superimaginary numbers. Nevertheless we put them into the series because we are led to see that they are necessary if we wish to formulate in an orderly way what happens in the realm of chemical activity, light, heat, and what takes place in addition when we pass out in one direction through this series and come back into it from the other direction.

One who has the organ to perceive these things finds something highly remarkable here. He finds something which, I believe, furnishes a real foundation for illuminating the basic facts of physical phenomena. What I mean is this. The same sort of difficulty that meets one in the consideration of superimaginary numbers also meets one when the attempt is made to apply the science of the inorganic to the phenomena of life. It cannot be done with these concepts of the inorganic. They simply do not apply. What has been the result of this? On the one hand there are thinkers who say, "The organic things of the earth have arisen by spontaneous generation out of the inorganic." But with this view alone one can never connect with something real. Other thinkers, like Preyer,[52] regard the organic as the source of everything inorganic, and they come nearer to the truth. They think of the earth as originally a living body, and what is inorganic today they consider as something precipitated out, as something that has died out of the organic. But these people do not make us an entirely satisfactory picture.

The same difficulty that meets us in the phenomena of nature considered by and for themselves is met also when we attempt a comprehensive mathematical formulation of what is present in the realms of heat, light, and chemical activity and what is arrived at when we attempt to close the color band in a natural way. We must assume, of course, that this color band can be closed somewhere, although it is obvious that it cannot be done under terrestrial conditions.

It is necessary for us to recognize how the purely mathematical leads up to the problem of life. With the facilities at hand today you can handle the phenomena of light, heat, and chemical action, let us say, but you cannot handle what is evidently connected with these, namely the closing off of the spectrum, which cannot be expressed by the same kind of formulae.

It will be helpful to us at this stage if we establish a terminology, but now we can base this terminology on concrete concepts. We have said: something real is at the basis of the formula for w. Let us speak of this as *warmth ether*. Likewise something real is involved when we change the positive signs of the heat formula to negative ones, and here we speak of the chemical ether. When it is necessary to use imaginary numbers in our formulae, we speak of the *light ether*. And we speak of *life ether* when we need to use mathematical formulae that we actually don't have yet and concerning which we are very unclear, mathematically speaking, just as the natural scientists are unclear regarding the nature of life.

You can see here an interesting parallelism between the course of thinking in mathematics and that within natural science itself. The parallelism shows how we are really dealing not so much with an objective difficulty but rather with a subjective one. For the purely mathematical difficulty arises of itself, and independently of the science of external things. No one would believe that a beautifully built lecture could be delivered on the boundaries of mathematical thinking, similar to the one Du Bois-Reymond[53] delivered on the boundaries of natural science. The conclusions would be different, at least. Within mathematics – unless the matter eludes us because it is too complicated – in this realm of the purely mathematical it must be possible to set up a complete formulation. The fact that one cannot do this is connected with our own relative lack of maturity. It is unthinkable that we have here a real boundary or limit to human knowing. It is extremely important that you pay strict attention to this. For this shows us that we cannot resort to a simple application of mathematics if we say, as energeticists do, for instance, that "a quantity of heat changes into a certain quantity of chemical energy and vice versa." This we cannot do; rather we are required to bring in certain other kinds of numerical values when a process like this takes place. The matter requires that we see as the most essential aspect not the quantitative mechanical change from one energy to another but rather a truly qualitative transformation. This may well be expressed mathematically when one form of energy, as it is said, passes over into another.

If people turned their attention to these qualitative changes that are already expressed by the numerical formulations, such ideas as the following would not be advanced: "Heat is what we experience as heat, mechanical energy is what we experience as mechanical energy, chemical energy is what we see as chemical processes; but within, these processes are all alike. Mechanical motion is manifesting everywhere, and heat is nothing but a form of this movement."

This idea of a bombardment, of collisions between molecules and atoms or between these and the walls of a vessel – this struggle for an abstract unity of all energy that makes it into a mechanical motion and nothing more – such things as these would not have arisen if it had been seen that even when we calculate we must take into account the qualitative differences between various forms of energy. It is very interesting in this connection to see how Eduard von Hartmann, when he considered the theory of heat philosophically, was obliged to find definitions for physics that excluded everything qualitative. Then one naturally finds nothing but a one-sided mathematics in physics. Aside from the cases where negative quantities arise from purely mathematical relationships, physicists do not like to reckon with numerical quality differences in physics. They use positive and negative signs, but only because of purely mathematical relationships. In the ordinary theory of energy, justification would never be found for the fact that there is a heat energy and a different energy, chemical energy, which can be designated with positive and negative signs on the basis of qualitative differences.

Lecture XIII

*Stuttgart,
March 13, 1920*

Today we will first carry out the experiments I had in mind yesterday, because they will lead us to a conclusion of our considerations for now. Tomorrow, I will try to conclude this series of lectures. We will now demonstrate completely adequately that within what we call the ordinary sun spectrum or light spectrum there are intertwined heat effects, light effects, and chemical effects. Yesterday we saw that the forces involved in the phenomena of life are also interlaced with these effects, only we are not able to bring these life effects into the field of our investigations in the same way as we can the chemical, light, and heat effects. For there is not yet a simple experimental method by which the twelvefold spectrum can really be shown in its effects. This will be the task of a research institute, working out of the insights of our movement, an institute where such investigations not only will be undertaken but pursued in detail.

Now I would like to call your attention to something. When we consider the hypothetical inclusion of life effects interlaced with heat, light, and chemical effects within our experimental approach, an important realm eludes us. This realm is physically more definitely manifested than the realm of the effects we have named. The realm that eludes us is that of acoustical effects, whose effects appear strikingly in the movements of the air, that is, in the movement of the gaseous or aeriform body. This brings up an important and fundamental question: how do we move on one side through the heat, light, and chemical spectrum to the life effects and on the other side to the acoustical effects?

This question presents itself simply through an overview of the whole field of phenomena; we can inform ourselves about it according to Goethean views of the physical world, as we have been doing up to now, rather than simply theorizing about it hypothetically.

Now let us try our first experiment.[54] When we place a solution of alum in the path of a light cylinder made into a spectrum by passage through a prism, we remove the heat effects from the spectrum. Let us first permit the thermometer to rise in consequence of the action of the heat effects within the spectrum. Then when we place the solution of alum in the path of the spectrum, we are able to observe a fall in the column of the thermometer. (The thermometer, which previously had been going up rapidly, rose more slowly.) The effect is shown by the fact that the thermometer rises more slowly. Therefore the alum solution removes the heat effects from the spectrum. We may consider this as proven – it has been done countless times and is a well-known fact.

The second experiment we will do is to insert in front of the path of the light cylinder a solution of iodine in carbon disulfide. You will see that the central portion of the spectrum is thereby entirely blotted out and the other portions considerably weakened. From the previous course you will remember that we have to consider this central portion essentially as that of the light effects. Thus, the light portion of the spectrum is stopped by the solution of iodine in carbon disulfide, just as the heat portion is stopped by the solution of alum. The thermometer now rises rapidly because the heat effect is present again.

The third thing we will do is to place a solution of aesculin in the path of the light cylinder. This has the characteristic of removing the chemical effects from the spectrum.

Thus we can influence the spectrum in such a way that we can remove the heat portion by means of an alum solution, the light portion by a solution of iodine in carbon disulfide, and the chemical portion by an aesculin solution.

We will establish the facts regarding the chemical effects by showing that when the chemical portion of the spectrum is active, a phosphorescent body glows. You can see that this body has been in the light cylinder, because when I block out the light momentarily with my hand, it glows. Now it must lose its glow through heat. We will place it again in the spectrum, but this time with the light cylinder passing through the aesculin solution. The result is very good. No phosphorescence is visible.

Now, keep in mind that we first have the realm of heat, the realm of light, and the realm of chemical effects. From our considerations taken in their entirety, you can conclude with at least a fair degree of certainty that a relationship must exist here to what I have pointed to in the past few days as the x, y, and z realms. In this way we are definitely approaching the point where we can gradually identify these realms.

Let us observe particularly the following. The heat realm, the x, y, and z realms, the gaseous, fluid, and solid realms, and the U realm are to be arranged as we have outlined. Recollect that there is, if we remain purely in the realm of phenomena, a certain very loose, mutual relationship to be observed between heat effects and phenomena manifested in a gaseous mass. We are able to observe that the gaseous body manifests in its material configuration what the heat is doing. The activity of heat can be found in its material expression in what the gas is doing. If we cultivate a vivid insight into what occurs in this interplay between gaseous matter and heat, between the heat effects and their material manifestation in the gaseous realm, we will also be able to get a real concept of the difference between the x realm and the realm of gases. We need only consider what we have seen countless times in life: that what we call light does not relate itself in the same way to gas as to heat. Gas does not follow changes in light by corresponding changes in its material configuration. When the light spreads out, the gas does not do likewise, it does not show a greater elasticity, etc.

Therefore when light is playing through a gas, the relationship is different from the one existing between gas and the heat playing through it. Now, in the observations made previously, we said: fluidity stands between gas and solid, heat between the x realm and the gaseous realm. Also the solid realm gives a picture of the fluid realm, the fluid realm gives a picture of the gaseous realm, and the gaseous realm gives a picture of the heat realm. So likewise we can say that the x realm can be a picture of heat, while heat is itself pictured in the gaseous realm. In the gaseous realm we have, as it were, pictures of pictures of the x realm.

Consider now that these pictures of pictures are really present when light passes through the air. Considering how the air relates itself with its various phenomena to light, one must say that we are not dealing with a direct picturing of one realm by the other; rather, the light actually has an independent status in the air in the gas. This independent relationship may be compared to the following: suppose we want to paint a landscape and hang the picture on the wall of this room and then photograph the room. By changing something in the room, I alter its whole appearance, and this alteration is evident in the photograph. If I were accustomed always to sit on this chair when giving a lecture, and some ill-disposed person removed it while I lectured without my noticing what he was doing, I would do what many have done under similar circumstances, namely, sit on the floor. The relation of things in the room undergoes real changes when I alter something in the room. But whether I hang the picture in one place or another, the relationship between the various figures painted in the picture does not change. What exists in the picture itself in the way of relationships is independent of alterations that go on in the room. In the same way, my experiments with light are independent of the air in the space in which they are carried out. Experiments with heat are, on the contrary, not independent of the space in which they are carried out, as you can easily convince yourselves; indeed, you are made aware of this by the whole room becoming warm. But my light experiments have an independent being; I can picture them in relief, as it were, so that when I experiment with x in an air-filled space, the same relationships prevail as when I experiment with light. I can identify x with light.

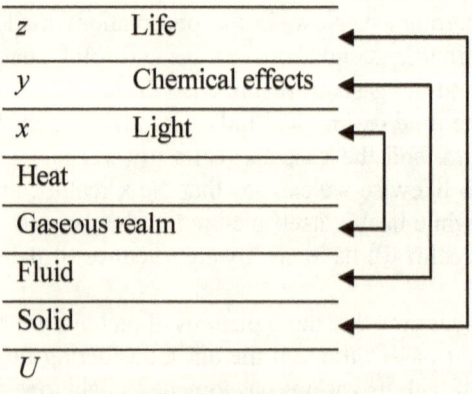

A further extension of this train of thought leads to the identification of y with chemical effects and of z with life effects. However, as you see, there is a certain independence between the light realm and the gaseous realm. The same sort of relationships are found if we extend the train of thought – you can do it for yourselves; it would lead us too far to do it here today – for instance, if we look for the chemical effects in the fluid realm. In fact, in order to call forth chemical action, solutions are always necessary. In these solutions chemical action is related to the fluid as light is to air, to the gaseous state. We then would expect to find the z realm associated with the solid. If I indicate the three realms by z, y, and x, with heat as the intermediate condition, I can then designate the gaseous realm with x', the fluid realm with y', and the solid realm with z'; I can represent the order like this:

$$z, y, x, \text{heat}, x', y', z', \text{ where}$$

x in x' represents light in gas,
y in y' represents chemical effects in fluids, and
z in z' represents the z effects in solid bodies. Formerly we knew them only as forms.

Thus we get interminglings, as it were, but these are nothing but conceptual expressions of things that are very real in our lives:

x in x' is simply light-filled gas,
y in y' is fluidity in which chemical processes are going on, and
z in z' is life effects acting in solids.

After yesterday's talk, you can scarcely doubt that just as we proceed beyond heat to find light, just as we proceed from light to find chemical effects, so beyond the chemical effects we must come to the life effects. This was spoken of yesterday, at least in a preliminary way. Therefore we may say that z in z' represents life effects in solid bodies. But there is no such thing as life effects in solid bodies. We know that under earthly conditions a certain degree of fluidity is necessary for life. Under earthly conditions life effects are not present in the purely solid state. But these earthly conditions force us to establish the hypothesis that such a condition is not beyond the realm of possibility, for the order in which we have been able to think of these things necessarily leads to this.

We find solid bodies, we find fluid bodies, we find gas. The solids we find without life effects. Life effects in the earthly sphere we only discover unfolding themselves adjacent to solid bodies, in relation to them, etc. But in the earthly realm we do not find a direct coupling of life effects with what we call solids. We are led to this last member of the series, z in z', life in the solid realm, by analogy with y in y' and x in x'. If I have a fluid body on the earth, it must have the same relation to chemical activity, although not so strong, as solid bodies do to life. Gases in the earthly realm must stand in the same relation to light as solids do to the living. Now, this leads us to recognize that in the earthly domain, solids, fluids, and gases in their supplementary relations to light, chemical action, and life phenomena represent something that has died out.

These thoughts cannot be made as obvious as people like to make most presentations of empirical facts. If you wish to make these facts really connect with reality, you must work them over within yourselves, and then, if you continue this sequence of thoughts, you will find that there is a kinship between the solid and the living, the fluid and the chemical, and the gaseous and light.

Heat stands as if set off by itself in a certain way. These relationships are not, however, directly expressed under earthly conditions. The relationships that can exist in the earthly domain point to something that was once there but is there no longer. Certain inner relationships in these things force us to bring time concepts into the picture. When you look at a corpse you are forced to bring in concepts of time. The corpse is there, but everything that makes possible the presence of the corpse, that gives it its appearance, all this you must consider as the soul-spiritual element, since the corpse has in itself no possibility of existence. The form of the human body would never arise without the soul-spiritual element. What the corpse presents to you forces you to say that what is there has been abandoned by something. This is no different from saying: the earthly solid has been abandoned by life, the earthly fluid by the emanations of the chemical effects, the earthly gaseous by the emanations of light effects. And just as we look back from the corpse to life, to the time when matter that is now the corpse was bound together with the soul-spiritual element, so we look from the solid bodies of the earth back to a former physical condition, when the solid was bound up with the living.

At that time the entire earth was not solid as we now understand the solid condition, just as little as was the corpse of today a corpse five days ago. Solids were not found in an independent state anywhere on the earth and only occurred bound to the living; fluid existed only bound to chemical effects and gases only bound to light effects. In other words, all gas had an inner glittering, an inner illumination, an illumination that showed a wave-like phosphorescence and darkening as the gas was rarefied and condensed. Fluids were not as they are today but were permeated by a continuous living chemical activity. And at the foundation of all was life, solidifying itself (as it solidifies now in the horn formation in cattle, for instance) and then passing back again into fluid or gas, etc. In brief, we are forced by physics itself to admit a previous period of time when realms now torn apart on the earth existed together. The realms of the gaseous, the fluid, and the solid are now found on one side, and on the other side realms of light, chemical effects, and life. At that time they were within each other, not merely side by side, but actually within each other.

Heat had an intermediate position. It did not appear to share this kinship of the material and the more etheric natures. But since it occupied an intermediate position, it is clearly conceivable that it participates in both the material and the etheric. If we now call the upper realm the etheric and the lower realm that of ponderable matter, we obviously have to consider the heat realm as the condition of equilibrium between them. Thus in heat we have found the condition of equilibrium between the etheric and the ponderable material realm. It is ether and matter at the same time and indicates by its dual nature what we actually find everywhere in heat, namely, a *difference in level*, an observation without which we cannot understand or arrive at anything in the realm of heat phenomena.

If you take up this line of thinking, you will come to something much more fundamental and important than the so-called second law of thermodynamics, that a perpetuum mobile of the second kind is impossible. For this second law really tears a certain realm of phenomena out of its proper connection; this realm is bound up with other phenomena and is essentially and profoundly modified by them.

If you make it clear to yourselves that the gaseous realm and the light realm were once one, that the fluid realm and the chemical effects were once one, etc., then you will also be led to think of the two polarically opposed portions of the heat realm – namely ether and ponderable matter – as originally united. That is to say, you must conceive of heat in former ages as completely different from heat as you think of it now. Then you will come to say to yourselves that the things we designate as physical phenomena today, only the expression of which is in the physical entity, are limited in their meaning by time. Physics is not eternal. For many completely different types of reality physics has absolutely no validity. For of course the reality in which gas was once directly illumined within is an entirely different reality from that in which gas and light are relatively independent in relation to one another.

Thus we come to look back on a time when another type of physics was valid; and looking into the future, there will be a time when a still different type of physics will be valid. Our modern physics can only conform with the phenomena of the present time, with what is in our immediate environment. In order to avoid paradoxes, and not only these but absurdities, physics itself must be freed of the tendency to study physical phenomena from our earthly domain, build hypotheses based on them, and then apply these hypotheses to the whole universe. We apply our earthly hypotheses to the universe and forget that what we know as physical is limited by time to the earthly domain. That it is limited in space we have already seen, for the moment we move out to the sphere where gravity ceases and everything streams outward, at that moment our entire physical view of the world ceases to apply.

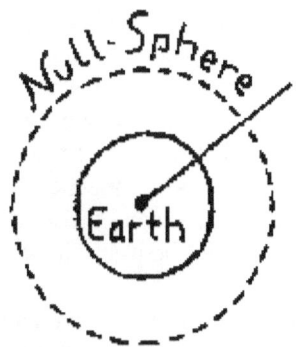

We have to say, therefore, that our earth is not simply spatially limited but that it is spatially limited in its physical qualities. It is nonsensical to suppose that beyond the null-sphere (see drawing) something will be found to which the same physical laws must apply. It is just as nonsensical to apply the same physical laws to former ages and to derive the nature of earthly evolution from what is going on at a particular time. The madness of the Kant-Laplace theory consists of the belief that it is possible to abstract something from contemporary physical phenomena and extend it arbitrarily backward in time. Modern astrophysics also shows the same madness in the belief that what can be abstracted from earthly physical conditions can be applied to the constitution of the sun, for example, and that we can speak about the sun on the basis of the earthly physical laws.

But something tremendously important presents itself to us if we take this overview of the phenomena that we have gained and then bring together certain series of phenomena. Your attention has been called to the fact that physicists have come to a view neatly expressed by Eduard von Hartmann. The second law of thermodynamics states that whenever heat is changed into mechanical work some heat remains unchanged, and thus, finally, all energy must change into heat and the earth come to a heat death. This view has been expressed by Eduard von Hartmann as follows: "The world process has the tendency to run down."[55] Now suppose we assume that such a running down of the world process does take place in the direction indicated, what happens then?

When we conduct experiments to illustrate the second law of thermodynamics, we see that heat appears; we see mechanical energy used up and heat appearing. What we see appearing undergoes a further change. For we can show likewise, when we produce light from heat, that not all of the heat reappears as light, since heat simply reverses the mechanical process as it is understood in the sense of the second thermodynamic law. It is similar with the relationship between light phenomena and chemical phenomena.

This has led us, however, to say that we have to imagine the whole cosmic spectrum as bent around into a circle. Thus if it were really true, as examination of a certain series of phenomena indicates, that the entropy of the universe is striving to reach its maximum and that the world process is running down, provision is also made for it to run back. It runs down here on this side but then runs back from here (indicating figure) on the other side, for we have to think of it as a circle.[56] Thus even if the heat-death actually occurs on one side, on the other side there occurs something to reestablish the equilibrium and that opposes the world's death with universal creation. This follows from a sober observation of the phenomena.

This can be verified in physics if it no longer observes the world process as we usually look at the sun's spectrum, going off into infinity in the past on one side, as we follow the red into infinity, and going into infinity in the future on the other side, as we follow blue into infinity. Instead we must symbolize the world process with a circle, and only in this way can we draw near to the world process.

Once we have symbolized the world process as a circle, however, then we can include in it what lies in our various realms. But we have had no opportunity to include the acoustic phenomena in these realms. These do not lie in *that* plane, as it were. In them we have something new, and we will speak further of this tomorrow.

Lecture XIV

*Stuttgart,
March 14, 1920*

By giving you just a few indications today, I will try to bring these considerations to a close for the time being. It is obvious that what we have sought for in the former course and in this one can only emerge fully when we are in a position to extend our treatment of the subject further. I will make a few remarks on these things at the conclusion of today's lecture.

First let me give a general summary of what we have considered in connection with heat phenomena and everything connected with them. Out of the array of concepts you have gained, I will draw your attention to certain ones. If we picture once again the realms of reality that we are able to distinguish in physics, we may list them as follows: The solid realm, which we have called z'; the fluid realm, which we have called y'; the *gaseous* or *aeriform* realm, denoted by x'. Between them we then had the warmth realm, had x as the light realm, y as the realm of chemical effects, and by z we have denoted the realm of life effects.

z	Life effects	
y	Chemical effects	← Tone Effects
x	Light realm	←
	Warmth	
x'	Gaseous	←
y'	Fluid	← Chemical process
z'	Solid	
	U	

Moreover, we considered yesterday very definite relationships that arise concerning the heat realm when we pass from x to x' and from y to y'. We tried, for example, to present to you facts that showed how chemical effects are able to realize themselves in the fluid element. One who strives to comprehend chemical processes finds that wherever chemical processes are taking place, everything having to do with chemical combinations and chemical dissociations or dissolutions is connected with the fluid element in a certain way. The fluid element must be allowed to work in its own particular way into the solid or gaseous realms in order for the chemical effects to occur. Thus when we speak about our earthly chemistry, we must keep in mind an interpenetration of chemical effects and the fluid element, with a relative separation of these two realms, and with this interpenetration, a kind of mutual binding of chemical effects and the fluid realm. Our earthly chemistry therefore presents to us the enlivening of the fluid element, as it were, by chemical effects.

You will readily conceive, however, that when we consider these various realms of reality it is impossible for us to think that this working of one realm into another is limited to the activity of heat in the gaseous realm. The other realms also work within each other. The other realms call forth certain effects in this or that field of action. Indeed, we can say that, although chemical effects work primarily in the fluid medium since they have an inner kinship to it, we must also picture the working of chemical effects in x', for example, that is to say a direct working of chemical effects in the gaseous or aeriform element.

When I say "chemical effects" you must not think only of chemical processes. You must think of something that comes to clear manifestation in the blue-violet portion of the spectrum and is penetrated with an inner spiritual element. Here we have the chemical effects revealing themselves somewhat independently in relation to material existence. When we speak of chemical processes, however, we are really dealing with the chemical effects as they interpenetrate the material realm. We must conceive of something here in this chemical realm that to begin with has nothing to do with ponderable matter but interpenetrates it;

in particular it interpenetrates the fluid element owing to an inner kinship with it, whose character I showed you yesterday.

But let us now ask ourselves what happens when this chemical effect picks out (figuratively speaking) the next element, the gaseous, for its activities? Then – if we stick with what is perceptible – something arises in the gaseous realm that shows a certain relationship to the manifestation of this effect in the fluid element, something that can be compared to this manifestation. In the fluid element, the chemical effect seizes upon matter, as it were, and so stirs the matter that a mutual interaction of constituent materials themselves occurs. When we picture the fluid element, we must think that the materials in it enter into mutual interaction during the chemical processes.

Let us assume, however, that the action does not reach the point where the chemical effect lays hold of the matter itself; rather let us assume that it works on the matter from the outside only, that it remains a bit more removed from the matter than is possible in the fluid medium; then something reveals itself as a side effect of the chemical effects more strongly in the gaseous realm than in the fluid. Then a certain independence arises of the imponderable compared with the material carrier. In chemical processes proper, the imponderable lays hold strongly of the material. Here, however, we come upon realms where there is not such a strong connection, where the imponderable does not remain within matter: this is the case in the acoustical realm, with the effects of tone. While in chemical-material processes we have a complete immersion of the imponderable in matter, in tone we have a persistence, a self-preservation, of the imponderable in gaseous or aeriform matter. This leads us further. It leads us to the point at which we have to say: there must be a reason that in fluids the imponderable seizes directly on the material, while in tone effects arising in the gaseous realm the imponderable is less able to do this.

If we observe chemical activity and have a feeling for what is to be seen within the physically visible, then we will become aware as a matter of course that it is simply in matter's nature for chemical phenomena to proceed as they do. That is to say, the imponderable is there as something characteristic of matter. This is possible only due to the fact that when we are dealing with earthly matter, the imponderable lays hold of matter through the earth. By means of the forces of the earth, the chemical effect is taken hold of, as it were, and works within fluid matter. You see the forces of form extended over the whole earthly realm and active by virtue of the fact that these forces of form master the approaching chemical effect.

When we really understand correctly that here we have the force of the earth, then we must assume the reverse force if we wish to comprehend correctly the weaving of tone in the air. That is, we have to think of forces active in tone that pass into the earth from all directions of the cosmos, forces that have a tendency to overcome the earth, therefore removing the imponderable from the earth. This is the peculiarity of the tone world. It is this that gives the particular characteristics to the physics of tone, of acoustics. In this realm we can on the one hand study the material processes physically, and on the other hand we can live in the world of tone with our feelings without paying the slightest attention to acoustics. What does acoustics matter to us as sensitive human beings when we perceive tone? Acoustics is a beautiful science because it reveals to us striking inner laws and an inner order, but what lives in us as a subjective experience of the world of tone is far, far removed from the physics of acoustics as it is expressed in the material world.

This is simply due to the fact that the tone element preserves its individuality; it reveals its origin to us, showing itself as determined from the periphery of the universe, while the chemical processes active in fluid matter show themselves as determined from the center of the earth.

One relationship was described beautifully in Dr. Kolisko's[57] lecture yesterday; this relationship shows itself only when we rise to a universal point of view, as it were. Then we can conceive of the periodic arrangement of the elements in octaves. Here we have an analogy between the inner lawfulness of tone and the entire structure of matter as it prepares to develop chemical processes.

By this means it is established that we may conceive all the combinations and breaking down of material existence as an outer reflection of an inner world music. This inner world music reveals itself to us outwardly in earthly music only in a particular case. This earthly music should never be regarded in such a way that we merely say: what is tone within us is only vibrating air outside of us. This must be looked upon as nonsense. It is just as nonsensical as if we were to say the following: what you are outwardly as a physical body you are as a soul when observed from within; such a statement leaves out the subject. Likewise we leave out the subject when we consider tone in its inner lawfulness as identical with the condensations and rarefactions of the air, which are the carrier of tone outwardly in the gaseous medium. Now if you consider this correctly, you will see that in chemical processes we have to do with a certain relationship between y and y', and in the activity of tone we have to do with a certain relationship between y and x' (see chart on page 165).

I have already indicated to you that when we remain within this or that realm what we become aware of in the outer world always pertains to a difference in level. Please try now to ascertain what is similar to a difference in level in the realm with which we are now dealing. Let us try to ascertain what is similar to a difference in level that becomes active in the case where gravity is used to furnish a driving force to push a wheel by means of falling water. Let us try to make clear to ourselves that we have differences in level involved in temperature, heat, tone, and in the equalization of electricity. Everywhere there are potential differences in level; we meet them wherever we study activity. But what do we have here? (See chart, page 165, arc $y - y'$.) We have an inner kinship between what we perceive in the spectrum and matter in the fluid state; what presents itself to us as a chemical process is nothing but the difference between chemical effects and the forces that are in the fluid. It is a difference in level, $y - y'$. And in the activity of tone we encounter a lesser difference in level, $y - x'$.

Thus we can say that in relating a chemical process to the realms of reality we are dealing with a difference in level between chemical-effects and fluid forces. In the manifestation of tone and sound in the air, we are dealing with a difference in level between what is working in a formative way in the chemical effects, beginning from outside at the periphery and shooting through the world, and the material of the gas, the aeriform body. What expresses itself in this realm of reality also expresses itself by means of differences in level. These things depend on differences in level even when we remain in *one* element, in warmth, or even in gas or water. Especially in perceiving distinctions between realms, however, we find we are dealing with differences in level of the effects of these realms.

Taking all of this together, you arrive at the following: from a consideration of fluidity and its relative surfaces, we are obliged to attribute the form of solids to earthly forces. The extent to which formative forces – the energies of configuration, to borrow an expression from modern physics – are related to gravity has been suggested to you in previous lectures. If we proceed from the forces that manifest as gravity to those that result in liquid surfaces – apparently planar surfaces due to the tremendous size of the earth – we find we are really dealing with a sphere. Obviously the different surfaces of all the terrestrial bodies of water taken together constitute a sphere. Now you will see that when we move outward from the center of the earth toward the surface of the sphere, we meet successively different sets of conditions. For earthly relationships within the solid realm we have to do with forces that tend to enclose, to delimit. Forces within fluidity, however, may perhaps be represented in their configuration by a line or plane tangential to the surface of the sphere (see drawing on p. 171). If we proceed out further and observe the realm of the sphere from without, then we must describe the situation in this way: beneath this sphere we have to do with the formative forces of our solid bodies, with formative forces that on the earth itself delimit the spatial body. Here (the colored sphere in the drawing), the many different forms together unite to create a single form, interpenetrate as it were to create the form of the earth's fluid element. How must we picture the situation, however, if we move out to here (outside the sphere)? For we have passed beyond what is formed individually, beyond what is shaped from within as the solid bodies are, so that the whole has a form. How must we picture this to ourselves? Well, we must imagine that we have the opposite condition. Here (drawing on left), we have solids filled out with matter; here, then, we must have space filled with negative matter (drawing on right). Here on the left we have filled space, and here on the right the opposite condition, space emptied out.

Filling of Space   Emptying of Space

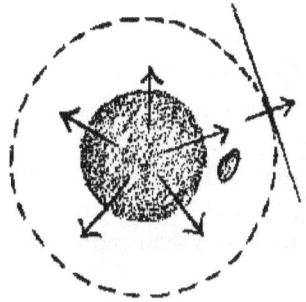
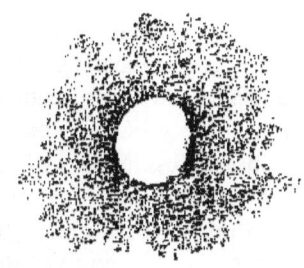

It must become possible for human beings to picture that an emptying of space is possible. Furthermore, what happens on the earth is indeed influenced not only by what happens from one side but by effects from all sides. If this were not so, earthly processes themselves would be entirely different. This can only be mentioned today; later we will go into it more thoroughly. It would not be possible, for example, for us to have a separation of continents from bodies of water, or the difference between the north and south poles, if in the environment of the earth there were only one such hollow space. These "matterless" spaces must work in from various directions. If we search for them, we find them in what the older cosmic systems designated as the planets, to which we must also add the sun itself.

Thus we are forced from the realm of the earth into the realm of the cosmos, and we are obliged to find the transition from one side of space to the opposite side. We must find the transition from a space filled with matter to one emptied of matter. This condition of space emptied of matter, in so far as it acts on our earth, we must think of as localized in the planets surrounding the earth. Thus at every point where earthly events can take place, there is a mutual interaction between the earthly and the cosmic; and this is due to the fact that from the spaces emptied of matter a suction-like effect is active, while in what is active here through the formative forces there are effects of pressure.

This mutual interaction meets us in those configurations of earthly events ordinarily sought for in molecular forces and attractions. We would be much better off, however, conceiving of these things as they were thought of by the intuitive knowledge of former times. Manifestations in matter, which are always accompanied by the imponderable, were then thought of as influenced by the whole cosmos instead of being misinterpreted as due to certain theoretical inner configurations. What the stars, like giants, do in presenting their many-sided relationships in earthly processes, is given expression by the dwarves of atoms and molecules. Indeed, what is necessary is for us to know that when we represent a material, earthly process or perform calculations on it, we are dealing with nothing other than an image of extraterrestrial, of cosmic interactions.

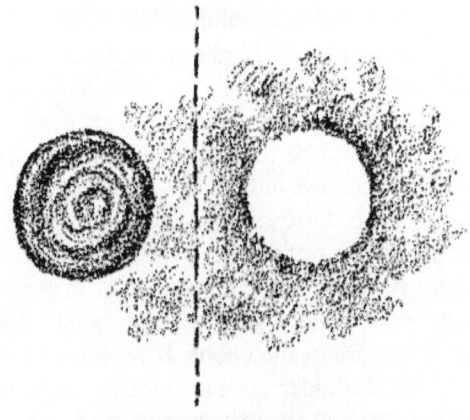

Here we have the force that fills space with matter (see drawing, left). Here (drawing, right) we still have this force that fills space with matter, but this force is spread out, and somewhere it must arrive on the other side, it must ultimately come to the condition where there is an emptying of space. And there must be a region in between where space is torn apart, if I may express it in this way.

We must say to ourselves that our space, which appears to surround us and is the vessel for physical manifestations, must have an inner relationship to physical activity. Something in our space must correspond to what is within this physical actvity. But when we go from the ponderable into the imponderable, space is torn apart. And in this tearing apart, something enters through the tear that was not there before it happened. Let us assume that we tear apart three-dimensional space. What is it that enters through the tear? When I cut my finger blood comes out – it remains within three-dimensional space. If I tear apart space itself, however, what emerges through the tear is something that is already within the nonspatial.

We can see that modern physical thinking is lost in the woods. When we do electrical experiments in the classroom, our electrical apparatus must be painstakingly dried, we must insulate it well, or our experiments will fail, won't they? If it is moist, the experiment will fail. I have often called attention, however, to the fact that, according to the physicists, the inner friction of clouds, which are certainly moist, is supposed to give rise to electricity, appearing in lightning and thunder.[58] This is one of the most impossible ideas conceivable.

On the other hand, if we pull together the things we have considered necessary for a real understanding of physical phenomena, then we can see that space is torn apart the moment the flash of lightning appears. At that moment, what fills space in an intensive way, not dimensionally, erupts like the blood when I cut my hand. This is always the case, in fact, when light appears accompanied by heat. Space is torn apart, space reveals to us what dwells within it, while it shows us only its outer side in the usual three dimensions that we have before us. When lightning flashes, space leads us into its inner content.

We may thus say that when we ascend from the ponderable to the imponderable, passing through the realm of heat as we go, we find the heat welling out wherever we make the transition from the pressure effects of ponderable matter to the suction effects of the imponderable. At all such points of transition, heat wells out.

You will see now that when we construct ideas about the processes we spoke of several days ago as those of heat conduction, we have to relate to them the concept that this heat conduction is bound to ponderable matter. This is quite the opposite of what we have demonstrated as the radiating heat itself. The radiating heat itself we find as that which wells out when space is torn apart. How will this warmth be active? It will work out of the intensive condition of space into the extensive condition of space. It will, so to speak, work from the inner aspect of space into its outer manifestations. When heat and a material body mutually react on one another, we see something occur; what occurs is that the characteristic tendency of the heat is transformed. Its suction effect is transformed into a pressure effect, the cosmic tendency of the heat is opposed by the individualizing tendency of the material which, in solids, becomes the form-giving force.

In heat, therefore – in the manifestation of heat as it leads to heat conduction – we must look not for rays but for a tendency to spread out in all directions. We must look for a mirroring of imponderable matter in ponderable matter, or for the presence of the imponderable in ponderable matter. A body that conducts heat is continually bringing heat to manifestation by an intensive reflection of the impinging imponderable heat onto matter. This contrasts with the extensive reflection characteristic of light.

I would like to request that you work through in your minds the concepts we generally entertain, to work them through in the way we have done here so that you really find them becoming saturated with reality. Let me give you a final picture to recapitulate and show you how such reality-saturated concepts can lead us into a living comprehension of universal existence.

I have already called your attention to what the perception, the subjective experience, of temperature consists of. We are actually experiencing the difference between the temperature of our own organism and that of the environment, which, indeed, is what the thermometer does – I have drawn this to your attention. Now all perception consists of the fact that we are something within a certain realm, while what lies outside of this realm becomes our perception. We cannot be a thing and perceive it at the same time; we must always be something different from what we are .perceiving. Suppose we perceive tones: in so far as we perceive tones, we cannot be the tones themselves. What are we as perceivers of tones? If we are to answer this question impartially, we come to the conclusion that we are something on a different level from what we perceive. We perceive the $y - x'$ difference in level; we do not perceive the $y - y'$ difference, because at this time we *are* that difference in level (see chart, page

165). This difference accompanies our perception of tone as inner chemical processes occurring regularly in our fluid organism; these are part of our being. What causes chemical effects within us produces certain orderly effects in the world itself. It is by no means without interest to consider the following picture. You know well that the human body consists of only a small portion of solid constituents; more than 90 per cent of it is a column of fluid. What plays through our organism in the very delicate chemical processes while we listen to a symphony is an inner, continually phosphorizing marvel. We are in our inner nature what these chemical processes reflect from tone. And we perceive tone through the fact that we become the tone world chemically in the sense I have described to you.

Our understanding of the human being is essentially broadened, you see, if we bring an understanding of physical problems to bear on the human being. What we must strive for, however, is not to form the abstract concepts of which physics is so fond today. Rather, we must penetrate through to the concepts that are really woven into the world, the objective world. Fundamentally, everything that spiritual science is striving to bring into the conceptual world, and especially what it is striving to do to foster a certain way of thinking, has as its object to bring back into human evolution thinking that is permeated with reality. And it is indeed necessary for this to happen. We must therefore pursue vigorously studies such as those that have been presented here during the last few days.

You can see how everywhere around you something old is dying away. From our examination of physical concepts we can see that something old is really dying away, for little can be done with them. And doesn't the fact that we can build up a new approach to the physical – even if we attempt it in such a limited way, for we can give only indications now – doesn't this fact show us that we stand today at a turning point in human evolution?

We must always be aware that we need to push forward the various lines of endeavor that Dr. von Baravalle, Dr. Blümel, Mr. Strakosch,[59] and Dr. Kolisko have presented to you in order to give a new impulse to the evolution of the human race. In this way we will lay foundations for progress. People all over the world are asking for something to be built up, for the construction of public schools, for example. But what does it mean that people are calling for these schools? The Danish school movement should tell us something. What is characteristic of the old schools is simply being carried into the new ones. But nothing new will come of this. It just means that soon everyone will be infected by the same ailment that up to now has infected only the educated few.

Nothing is sadder than to contemplate a future in which the way of thinking that has devastated the minds of educated people will be transmitted to people throughout the whole earth by means of the public school system. If one wishes to found schools for the people, we must be sure that there will be something to teach in them, something whose inner configuration represents an advance. We first need the science that could be taught in these new schools. People always prefer to remain superficial, considering only what is obvious. People in politics never want anything new but prefer to stick to the old. Just as the Social Democrats aren't building anything new, but stick to the old type of state, just wanting to put in their two cents there, so those in movements to renew culture don't really want to strive for a renewal of our way of thinking but simply want to carry the old and decaying way to the people. This tendency is most noticeable in the physical sciences.

You will certainly find many things in these lectures that are unsatisfying, for I could only offer initial suggestions at best. One thing is clearly shown in these lectures, however, and that is the necessity to build anew our whole physical, chemical, physiological, and biological approach to the world. It must be rebuilt from the ground up. We will accomplish this not only when we have developed further not just the schools but the nature of science itself. And until we have succeeded in the Waldorf schools to the extent that the subjects for instruction have been renewed along the lines begun seminally in these last few days, only then will we achieve what should and must be achieved if European civilization is not to perish spiritually.

Just consider the shocking trend in the modern academic world. Long, controversial papers are read, completely divorced from real life. People sit in fine lecture halls, and each reads his long, drawn-out lecture. And the others don't bother to listen, for one man is a specialist in one area, another man is a specialist in another. The mathematician lectures, but the medical man does not listen. And when the medical man lectures, the thoughts of the mathematician are busy elsewhere. This is indeed a well-known and traditional state of affairs. Something new must be implanted here. And this something must have its center in spiritual striving. This must be understood. If we can but bring together this striving toward a new kind of reality with building up a new way of thinking in our schools, we will achieve what must be achieved.

You can see that there is much to be done. We really learn how much is to be done only when we begin to go into details. It is therefore pathetic that people today who cling to the old way of thinking – for it has become old, it has had its day – change only the way it is phrased; they accumulate large amounts of capital to perpetuate their academic system in the world. It is especially difficult because we must be permeated by the conviction that something genuinely new is necessary. We must not surrender to illusions and simply say, "Build schools for the people." We must live in reality and say, "First it is necessary to have something new to teach in these schools for the people." And while fruitful technological results have flowed from science up until now, I would like to suggest that a still more fruitful technology will flow from spreading a science of the nature we have tried to indicate here, for example, in the realm of physics.

In every case here we have tried to emerge from the old theoretical point of view and to approach reality itself, so that our concepts will be saturated with reality. This will yield technological results quite different from those attained up to now. Practice and theory are inwardly connected. If we see in any one case what kind of reform is needed, as in the case of physics, we can understand what must happen.

Since the time has come for us to part now, I would like to emphasize that I have only suggested some things to you in these lectures to stimulate you to develop these things further. You will be able to develop them. The mathematical physicists we have among us will be able to give new life to the old formulae.

And they will find, when they apply to these old formulae the ideas I have just indicated to you, that certain transformations can be experiences that are actual metamorphoses. A great deal will grow out of these metamorphoses that will be of enormous importance technically for the further evolution of humanity. This is something that cannot yet be gone into in detail but can only be indicated at this time.

These considerations must now be brought to a close, and their further progress will depend on your own work. I wish you to take this especially to heart, for things are now extremely pressing that have to be accomplished for humanity's progress in all three realms.[60] These things have become urgent in our era, and there is no time to lose because chaos stands at the door. A second thing to remember is this: the proper end can be attained satisfactorily only through people working in an orderly way together. Thus we must try to work out further, among ourselves, the things that have been stimulated here. On the other hand, you will also find something arising here in the work of the Waldorf School: the moment you really try to apply in your teaching the definite and valid concepts we have gained here, they will be taken up at once. You will also discover that they will work well if you find it necessary to apply them in the management of life.

It would be nice if we did not always have to speak about natural science to a public which, while it accepts much, is always exposed to the opinions of "rigorous scientific thinkers," of "authorities." These authorities have no inkling that everything we observe is continuously permeated by everything else. We can see this even from language.

In language, you see, we allow everything to be mutually interrelated. We speak of an impact. Now it is only because we have *ourselves* initiated the impact and given a name to the phenomenon that we speak of an impact in space free of human activity; the reverse is also true, that we speak of things that happen within us in words drawn from the outer world. We do not realize, however, that we should look into the outer world, into the planetary world for example, if we want to understand the constitution of earthly bodies. If we don't know this, we are also unable to learn about the origin of anything else. We discover all sorts of interesting things if we focus our microscopes on the embryos of plants and animals or any microscopic cell; we discover all sorts of interesting things there, but the source of all this, the thing we long to discover, we will be able to see only when we understand macroscopically the same processes we behold microscopically. We must see that fertilization and fructification take place continually in a mutual interaction with outer nature; we must learn how to conceive of the planets as points of departure for understanding the working of the imponderable in the physical world; we must see the cosmos as the starting point for the plant and animal germ cells; we must consider everything in the larger context that today we look for in the small context of a cell, viewed through a microscope; we must be able to look first to what surrounds us if we are to make any progress.

The way is now clear before us, but human prejudice is a very, very serious hindrance. This prejudice is difficult to overcome. It is our task to do everything we can to overcome it.

Let us hope that we can continue these considerations in the future.[61]

Notes

(Provided by the editors of the German edition of *The Warmth Course*)

1. This refers to the first natural scientific course, *The Light Course*, given December 23, 1919 to January 3, 1920 (GA Bibl.-Nr. 320).
2. The experiment with three vessels containing water at various temperatures was already familiar to Locke and Berkeley. Ernst Mach also described it in 1896 in his book on heat. He, however, used the same experiment to connect thoughts the opposite of those expressed here. The experiment is repeated even now in contemporary physics textbooks to demonstrate the supposed unreliability of sense perception.
3. *Zeno* (approximately 490-430 B.C.). Student of Parmenides. According to Aristotle, he discovered dialectics.
4. See note 1.
5. *Albert Einstein* (1879-1955). Founded the "Special Theory of Relativity" in 1905 and in 1915 the "General Theory of Relativity."
6. The meeting of the German Physics Society in Berlin had taken place only ten days before this lecture, on February 20, 1920. Max v. Lau presented a copy of a photograph made by English scientists during the total eclipse of the sun in Brazil on May 29, 1919. According to the general theory of relativity, those stars visible in the immediate vicinity of the sun were to appear diverted by the gravity of the sun. The values presented largely confirmed this theory. The discussion following that presentation, which is of special interest here, cannot be found in the proceedings of the German Physics Society. Evidently Rudolf Steiner referred to them here on the basis of newspaper reports, but this has not yet been able to be confirmed. Yet many other discussions of the general theory of relativity were included in the Society proceedings, occasioned in 1920 by the English eclipse expedition. This provides elucidation of the basis on which these discussions took place, e.g., A. Sommerfeld's paper, "Concerning the General Theory of Relativity and its Proof in Experience" (*Archiv für Elektrotechnik*, Vol. 9). In the solar spectrum the spectral lines in comparison with the spectra of earthly light sources appear shifted toward the red, apparently as a consequence of the sun's force of attraction. This shift is so slight, however, that it had not been noted until this time, and it lies at the limit of the available apparatus' capacity. In 1920, however, it was believed that such shifts had been demonstrated.
7. In certain ways *The Light Course* itself, cited in note 1, yielded examples of such confirmations. Rudolf Steiner was very interested in this matter not in order to confirm the theory of relativity as such; rather he was interested in the possibility of influencing colors in the spectrum by outer forc-

es. *The Warmth Course* itself leads to this problem in the eleventh and twelfth lectures.

8. Not much attention is directed today to the significant literature concerning such an approach at the end of the nineteenth and beginning of the twentieth centuries. A few examples follow:

Ernst Mach, *The Analysis of Sensation*, Dover Publications, New York, NY (translated by C.M. Williams): "We must regard it as an additional gain that the physicist is now no longer overawed by the traditional intellectual constructs of physics. If ordinary 'matter' must be regarded merely as a highly natural, unconsciously constructed mental symbol for a relatively stable complex of sensational elements, much more must this be the case with the artificial hypothetical atoms and molecules of physics and chemistry. The value of the constructs for their special, limited purposes is not one whit destroyed. As before, they remain economical means of symbolizing experience. But we have as little right to expect from them, as from the symbols of algebra, more than we have put into them, and certainly not more enlightenment and revelation than from experience itself. We are on our guard now, even in the province of physics, against overestimating the value of our symbols. Still less, therefore, will the monstrous idea of employing atoms to explain psychical processes ever get possession of us; seeing that atoms are but the symbols of those peculiar complexes of sensational elements that we meet with in the narrow domains of physics and chemistry.

"...Now if we resolve the whole material world into elements which at the same time are also elements of the psychical world and as such are commonly called sensations; if, further, we regard it as the sole task of science to enquire into the connection and combination of these elements that are of the same nature in all departments, and into their mutual dependence on one another; we may then reasonably expect to build a unified monistic structure upon this conception and thus to get rid of the distressing confusions of dualism. Indeed, it is by regarding matter as something absolutely stable and immutable that we actually destroy the connection between physics and physiology.

"...Not long after the first edition of this book was published (1885), I was lectured by a physicist on the misguided way in which I had conceived my task. In his opinion it was impossible to analyze the sensations as long as the paths of the atoms in the brain were unknown; and when they were known everything else would follow of itself. Of course I had not much use for utterances such as these which, had I been a young man of the period of LaPlace, might have fallen upon fertile ground and have developed into a psychological theory based on "concealed moments." The effect that they had was, however, to make me offer a silent apology to Du Bois-Reymond with his *ignorabimus* – a dictum that up to that moment I had regarded as the greatest mistake. After all, Du Bois-Reymond's recognition of the insolubility of his problem was an immense step in advance; this recognition removed a weight from many men's minds, as is shown by the success of his work, a success that is otherwise scarcely intelligible. He did not, indeed, take the further step of seeing that the recognition of a problem as insoluble in principle, must depend on a mistaken way of stating the question. For he too, like countless others, took the instruments of a special science to be the actual world."

Wilhelm Ostwald, *Overcoming Scientific Materialism*, a lecture held at the third general meeting of the Society of German Scientists and Physicians in Lübeck, September 20, 1895 (appearing in *Abhandlungen und Vorträge*, Leipzig, 1904): "Every scientifically thinking human being, be he mathematician or practicing physician, will formulate his views regarding the question of the 'inner aspect' of the world somewhat as follows: all things are constituted out of moving atoms, and these moving atoms and the forces working between them are the ultimate realities that constitute all isolated phenomena...I intend to express my conviction that this conception that is so universally assumed is untenable; that this mechanistic view of the world does not fulfill the purpose for which it was formulated, that it is in contradiction to incontestable and universally known and accepted truths. The conclusion that follows from this cannot be subject to doubt: the scientifically untenable view must be discarded and wherever possible be replaced by another better one... the inadequacy of the customary mechanistic view will be easier to verify than the adequacy of the new view that I would like to designate as the energetic view." (Compare this with Rudolf Steiner's comment on Ostwald in his book, *Goethean Science*.)

Georg Helm, *The Historical Development of Energetics*, (Leipzig, 1898): "...It has been pointed out repeatedly that into the 1880's thermodynamics was held to be intimately intertwined with the kinetic theory of gases, and hence with atomism. The thinking was that the law of energy and entropy provided a rough calculation that might well suffice for some purposes, for example, technical purposes, providing a useful tool similar to the center of gravity in mechanics, the area integral, or the energy integral. Such tools, however, never allow a pursuit of the intricacies of nature; they never open up a view into the mechanics of the inner aspect of bodies. Whoever dreams of the reduction of all phenomena to the movement of atoms as the highest goal of theoretical natural science may well think of thermodynamics...as a garbage theory, because it has access only to relationships that are late consequences of what he considers to be the actual and true innermost events. Overcoming this atomistic way of thinking is not the task only of energetics. More general intellectual efforts need to contribute to this. The achievement of energetics has been merely to unsettle the belief in the necessity of the atomistic hypothesis and the satisfaction it was to grant...It appears unnecessary to me today to rattle the sabers and move into battle against the mechanistic hypothesis; it has done its duty... What needs to be fought against is simply the attempt to bolster this mechanical hypothesis with all kinds of artifice, as if the existence of atoms were of greater importance than the simple description of experiences. Above all, however, a battle must be continued against the mingling of energetics with the molecular hypothesis, an error that has by no means been eradicated.

"With his fundamental work in 1847, Helmholtz initiated this mingling of the ideas about energetics with the molecular hypothesis. Robert Mayer holds himself completely free of these, and also in England, under the continuous influence of William Thomson, energetics has developed in a purer form. In Germany the gradually growing predominance of the mechanical hypotheses can be seen very clearly in the personal development of Clausius. In his first work of 1850...energetics is considered as a new science in addition to mechanics, but in the later works the molecular hypothesis increasingly predominates. Correspondingly, the entire course of scientific development in Germany from the mid-1850's to the 1880's appears to be a departure from the pure clarity of Mayer's intuition...

"As we follow the historical development, we encounter the work of Gibbs, entirely liberated from preconceptions concerning the mechanical view of atoms and fully determining the strict consequences of both main principles without always longing for or furtively glancing toward mechanics. Here the grand old thought of Robert Mayer has become alive in mathematical formulae, free of all molecular-hypothetical elaborations.

It is quite a book, in which chemical processes are treated without the handed-down chemical apparatus of atoms, in which the theories of elasticity, capillarity and crystallization, of electromechanical force, are presented without all the customary aid of atomistic origins! Naked and pure, the true object of the theoretical knowledge of nature stands before us...No wonder people did not understand Gibbs' work, despite the fact that Maxwell emphatically pointed out its significance."

9. *Rudolf Clausius* (1822-1888). German theoretical physicist. His treatises, originally published in *Poggendorffs Annalen*, are published also in three volumes, *Die mechanische Wärmetheorie* (The Mechanical Theory of Heat), Braunschweig, 1876-1891. Especially noteworthy are the papers from 1850-56 in which the orientation is phenomenological and relates to the work of Carnot. In 1857 the atomistic theory of heat is introduced with the treatise called, "Concerning the Kind of Movement that We Call Heat."

10. For example, $1/273$ in gases at 0° C. By the same token, in earlier days other coefficients of expansion were expressed as fractions, for example, $1/81000$ for iron.

11. Refers here to gases that cannot be liquefied by pressure alone, in contrast to steam.

12. This image is not the usual kind of graphic presentation but rather something like a facsimile of the process: the curve rises when the temperature rises and remains stationary when the temperature remains constant.

13. *Sir William Crookes* (1832-1919). British physicist and chemist.

14. A sketch and more detailed explanations of this experiment are not available.
15. The transcriptions are not clear at this point concerning the relationship of the nature of warmth to pressure, to formative capacity and so on, and to temperature.
16. *Immanuel Kant* (1724-1804). See his "*How is Pure Mathematics Possible?*"
17. See Rudolf Steiner's *Knowledge of the Higher Worlds and Its Attainment*, (Anthroposophic Press, Spring Valley, NY, 1983) and *Spiritual Science, an Outline* (Anthroposophic Press, Spring Valley, NY, 1984). Also helpful is Steiner's presentation of this question in connection with natural science in the lecture cycle, *The Boundaries of Natural Science* (Anthroposophic Press, Spring Valley, NY, 1983), particularly lectures seven and eight.
18. See note 1
19. The word "difficulty" instead of "certainty" in the transcription was clearly an error of the stenographer, as many who have studied the course have noticed.
20. See Rudolf Steiner's *The Course of My Life* (Anthroposophic Press, Spring Valley, NY).
21. A loop of wire to which a weight is attached is placed around a horizontal ice block supported only at the ends.
22. With two parts bismuth, one part lead, and one part tin, the melting point is 94° C (this mixture is the so-called *Rose's metal*).
23. The transition in thought to the fluid state is indicated in the figure through the additional suggestion of the vessel drawn around the lines of fall and the surface level.
24. On page 25 water and ice were discussed as the "cardinal exception." This exception also applies to ice melting under pressure. There are very few other substances that behave similarly; they are the substances which, like ice, float while melting on the developing liquid, e.g., bismuth and gallium.
25. *Eduard von Hartmann* (1842-1906). Rudolf Steiner refers to him often, for example in his autobiography, *The Course of My Life* (Anthroposophic Press, Spring Valley, NY). Hartmann's main work was *The Philosophy of the Unconscious*, which stirred quite a sensation when it appeared in 1869. Von Hartmann later wrote about the various special realms of philosophy, but in individual works he also concerned himself with contemporary issues and the sciences. *The Worldview of Modern Physics* first appeared in 1902.
26. Soon after this course was given, the Scientific Research Institute was founded in Stuttgart within the framework of the corporation, *Der kommende Tag*, and this Institute had a section for physics. The difficulties that developed during the inflation in the 1920's resulted in that corporation being liquidated while Rudolf Steiner was still alive (1924). The ex-

periments undertaken as a further development of what was discussed in this course were thereby terminated, having had initial results that were partially successful. The possibilities for experimentation that existed at that time have never been duplicated since, and a few of these studies have never been adequately pursued.

27. The issue of the negative shape in contrast to the positive one is pursued more precisely later by Rudolf Steiner, particularly in *The Astronomy Course* (given from January 1-18, 1921), in which the word "antispace" (*Gegenraum*) was coined and indications were given concerning projective geometry. This course is not yet available in English.

28. "Free Waldorf School" refers to the first Waldorf School, founded by Emil Molt in Stuttgart in 1919 for the children of workers in his Waldorf-Astoria cigarette factory. This school was established under the guidance of Rudolf Steiner, initiating an educational movement that has since spread around the world.

29. This must have essentially reproduced the arrangements for experimentation established at that time. The purpose of the suction pump was to draw the air out of the condenser at the beginning of the experiment. This corresponds with an improvement that James Watt had introduced to the steam engine.

30. *Julius Robert Mayer* (1814-1878). German physician and physicist. His publications appear as a collection under the title, *Die Mechanik in der Wärme* (Stuttgart, 1867).

31. *Hermann von Helmholtz* (1821-1894). German physiologist and physicist. The treatise referred to here is *Über die Erhaltung der Kraft* (Berlin, 1847). The treatise begins with the words, "The derivation of the established principles can be attacked from two sides: either from the view that it would be impossible to gain an unlimited force for work through the interaction of a combination of natural forces, or from the assumption that all effects in nature tend to derive from attracting or repelling forces whose intensity depends only upon the distance between the interacting points."

32. See Goethe's *Lectures on Optics, Outline for a Theory of Color*, and "Confessions of the Author" in *Sources for a History of the Color Theory*. Also consult Rudolf Steiner's *The Light Course* (see note 1).

33. From Goethe's *Verses in Prose*: "This is why the human being is so elevated – because the unrepresentable is represented in him. What is a violin string and all mechanical division of it when compared with the ear of a musician? Yes, one could ask, what are the elementary phenomena of nature herself in comparison with the human being, who must first master and modify them in order to be able to assimilate them to some degree?" See Goethe's writings on natural science and Rudolf Steiner's book, *Goethean Science*.

34. J. R. Mayer wrote two papers, one in 1841 and another in 1842. The 1841 paper, *Concerning the Quantitative and Qualitative Nature of Forces*, was rejected without response by Poggendorff's *Annalen* and was published on-

ly after Mayer's death and is little known. Mayer's significance for physics began with the 1842 paper, *Remarks Concerning Forces in Inanimate Nature*. The 1842 paper was published in *Wohlers and Liebigs Annalen* on chemistry and pharmaceutics. The two papers are quite different in terms of their underlying thoughts. In 1841 Mayer was not yet able to relate his basic idea to the physics then in existence. Not so in 1842. Then he was able not only to establish this connection but also to calculate the heat equivalent from the Gay-Lussacs experiment and the specific heat of air. No other physicist of his time had suspected such a lawfulness underlying these facts. Looking back to 1841 in his autobiographical notes, Mayer writes, "At that time there were still erroneous ideas that disturbed the course of my thoughts, preventing me from coming to a clear view of the issues. In the physics of that time, in addition to the teaching of the parallelogram of forces, the term *mc* was given as a measure of movement. This term, connected with a remnant of concepts from the Kantian school of natural philosophy concerning centripetal and centrifugal force, led me into a labyrinth of hypotheses and contradictions...One can easily imagine that a system containing such absurdities and extravagances could not make a favorable impression upon the Tübingen professors to whom I presented this private publication in the summer of 1841. In the meantime, however, I continued to hold on to the fundamental idea of the equivalence of work and heat. It soon became evident to me that the *measure of movement* could only be determined by the square of the velocity and never by the simple velocity...so I did indeed succeed in giving my thoughts a more lucid form, and late in 1841 I could present my more clarified thoughts to Professor Jolly, who at that time was in Heidelberg...Professor Jolly approved of the presentation in general and encouraged me to pursue the matter further, to work it through and then publish it."

The submission of a paper to Poggendorffs *Annalen* in June 1841 is curiously not mentioned here at all. In the battle for recognition of Mayer's achievement, it played no role because it remained unknown. Mayer is quite humble in relation to *Poggendorff* and the other physicists when he speaks of his own "extravagances." Yet in confirmation of Rudolf Steiner's explanations, one needs to look also at what was overlooked at the time: the power of Mayer's idea that stood behind the totality, including the "extravagances."

35. *Johann Christian Poggendorff* (1796-1877). Editor of *Annalen für Physik and Chemie* from 1824-1877, in addition to being active in researching many areas of physics and chemistry. He developed various instruments and methods of measurement. An encyclopedia of physicists describes him by saying, "Poggendorff consistently placed primary worth on the experimental basis of science. He was no friend of idle speculations."

36. The existing drawing is difficult to understand without visualizing the process of drawing. Comparing the text with the variety of drawings found in the different sets of notes available yields the following. A blue, more-or-less rectangular surface represents the region from the gaseous down to

the solid state. In red upward and downward from that surface are the realms of warmth, x, y, z, and U. But these red "tails" are bent and drawn into the side of the blue area, most likely from the left to the right. A strong differentiation between left and right that can be seen in most notes, and also in the first edition, could be a result of repeated copying.

37. The captions to this drawing are found only in the notes of a participant in the course and were presumably added by him. They can nevertheless be helpful in understanding the drawing.
38. This sentence is followed in the transcripts only by the sentence, "But we must overcome this process," which does not really follow from the preceding sentence. A connecting sentence seems to be lost in the available notes. **See Addendum at end of notes.**
39. The discussion here repeatedly refers to a diagram that is missing in the course transcriptions. The one we give here has been taken from the previous lecture. What is missing is the further elaboration that most certainly occurred during this lecture.
40. Different readers of the course have come to a common picture when supplementing the diagram on page 124:

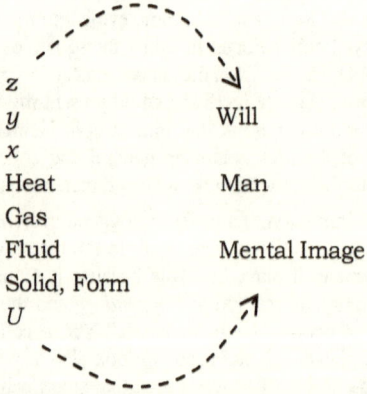

41. See note 1. Of particular interest is lecture five of *The Light Course*.
42. The drawing is missing, but it is evident from the discussion that an apparatus similar to the one described on page 120 was used, but now filled with ethyl alcohol instead of mercury.
43. *Eugen Dreher* (1841-1900). Rudolf Steiner summarized the sequence of experiments in a footnote to his comments on Goethe's natural scientific writings published in Berlin in 1897: "According to Goethe, Becquerel and Eugen Dreher have made valuable contributions to the study of 'luminous matter.' The brilliant comments by Dreher have given us especially lucid insights into the phenomena of luminous matter. Dreher exposed

green luminous matter (there is also blue-violet luminous matter, but it is less reactive) to light, to colorless sunlight as well as to light that had passed through various substances. He used 1) A colorless glass sphere containing a concentrated solution of aluminum potassium sulfate; 2) A similar sphere with a solution of iodine in carbon disulfide; 3) A similar sphere with a concentrated solution of aesculin; and 4) A sphere with distilled water. The results were that with 1) no warmth effects were evident; with 2) no light effects appeared; with 3) there were no chemical effects (for example, silver chloride does not turn black) within the space occupied by the spectrum. None of these effects took place in the fourth sphere. The luminous matter exposed to the light beam that passed through the aluminum potassium sulfate through water (1 and 4) showed in the dark a decisive luminosity (phosphorescence). The beam that passed through iodine and aesculin (2 and 3) showed no luminescence at all. Dreher then exposed matter that had been brought to luminescence to variously modified light beams. It became evident that under the influence of light that had passed through iodine and aesculin solutions, the luminosity initially became more intense but then ceased completely, while under the influence of light passing through aluminum potassium sulfate it persisted. The latter observation fully reinforces a fact that had been known for a long time, that luminous matter exposed to light for some time and in which luminosity has already ceased can be brought back to a state of luminescence – but only once – by warming the material. If the material then ceases to show luminescence, a second warming will only work once the material has been exposed again to light. It is evident from these observations that the capacity for luminescence (phosphorescence) of luminous matter is called forth by the same force that brings forth chemical effects. Heat is indeed able to bring forth luminescence, but it cannot give matter the capacity for luminescence; in fact, it destroys this capacity by bringing forth luminescence. For this reason, light masses that have been deprived of their chemical effect but not their warmth effect (having passed through an aesculin solution) first bring about luminescence and then a complete extinguishing of the phosphorescent body."

44. See note 1.
45. *Max Planck* (1858-1947). German theoretical physicist. The following discussion appears in Planck's lecture given September 23, 1910 during the 82nd meeting of German natural scientists and physicians in Königsberg: "In the lecture by Helmholtz, to which I referred initially, he especially emphasized that the first step in discovering the energy principle was that a question arose of what relationships must exist between the forces of nature for it to be possible to construct a perpetuum mobile. By the same token, it can justifiably be asserted that the first step toward discovery of the principle of relativity occurred with the question of what relationships must exist between the forces of nature if it were to prove impossible to demonstrate that light ether has any kind of material properties, if light waves progress through space without adhering to a material carrier. Then, naturally, the velocity of a moving body in relation to the light

ether could not be defined and certainly could not be measured. I don't need to emphasize that the mechanical view of nature is utterly incompatible with this point of view." (Max Planck, "The Relationship of Modern Physics to the Mechanical View of Nature," *Physikalische Abhandlungen und Vorträge, Braunschweig,* 1958.)

46. *Ernst Mach* (1838-1916).
47. *Jean Baptiste Joseph Fourier* (1768-1830). French mathematician, physicist, secretary of the Institut d'Egypte. His principal work was *Theorie Analytique de la Chaleur* (Paris, 1822).
48. This sentence preceded the brief comments following it, whose rendering in the transcripts is unclear. The significance of the word "effect" in the whole argument is not immediately obvious in connection with this. It may be intended very generally, having somewhat the same meaning as "process," here the "process of warmth conduction." However, it may mean something more definite, similar to the more accessible differentiation in the following lectures between "chemical effects" and "chemical processes."
49. In the original transcriptions, the formula was written with the square root sign covering the entire right side of the formula. But the formula is certainly trying to express simply that the value w has an imaginary quality. The context gives no clue that one is supposed to find the square root of the other terms, c or q, and the square root of the differential dt would be meaningless. The correction of the formula in this edition was attested to by various readers of the earlier edition. Here the fact is presented that the equation for the conduction of heat should be presented with an imaginary coefficient and therefore from a mathematical viewpoint. This formula represents the simplest version of the Schrodinger equations, but the equation for the conduction of heat is not presented as a differential equation of the second order but is simply a subtle reference to the work of Fourier. At the time when this formula was postulated, this formula would have appeared absurd to physicists. In 1926, Schrodinger postulated a similar equation in an entirely different context, using an analogy to wave optics to create wave mechanics. This became one of the bases for modern atomic physics.
50. The discussion took place following lectures by Dr. E. Blümel, "Concerning the Imaginary and the Concept of the Infinite and the Impossible," and by A. Strakosch, "Mathematical Structure as Intermediary Between Archetype and Image." Dr. Blümel asked, "Is it possible to arrive at a living perception of the imaginary realm? Do real entities lie at the basis of the imaginary?" Rudolf Steiner replied, "The answer to this question is not given so easily. The reason for this is that when one attempts to formulate the answer, one must leave the realm of the perceptible. It already became clear a few days ago, in answering Dr. Müller's question, that, in order to provide a perceptible correlate for a mathematical problem, I had to point to the transition of a long bone into a skull bone. Nevertheless, this is still

something entirely perceptible. At least in that realm the objects can be perceived, if only in a transition of one object into another.

"If one wants to look at the imaginary domain as spiritual reality, the following is required: an individual is forced, as I have just shown in these deliberations on physics, to pass over from the positive to the negative if he wishes to arrive at any kind of realistic conceptions concerning certain relationships of so-called ponderable matter to the imponderable. However, in trying to visualize even very ordinary realms, it already becomes necessary to get beyond the customary symbolic drawings. I will only give the following example. In drawing the ordinary spectrum in linear form, one can draw a straight line from red through green to violet; when drawn in this way, however, everything that should come into consideration is not contained in the symbolic image of the spectrum. Everything will be included only if, in order to symbolize red, a curve is drawn, moving approximately in this plane (sketch), and then, in order to reach the violet, the curve moves into and behind the blackboard so that if looked at from above the red would appear as if lying in front of the violet. With the red I would have to move forward and with the violet backward. This would then give me a picture of the violet's movement into the chemical realm and the red's movement away from it. I am thus forced to extend the straight line already here, so that the usual drawing of the spectrum is already a mere projection of what I should actually draw.

"In trying to attain clarity regarding certain matters that are simply facts in higher reality, it is not sufficient simply to pass from positive materiality to negative materiality. This would be just as unsatisfactory as moving in a straight line from red through green into violet. Think now of the circle drawn so that you will not, in moving from this point onward, return to the point where you started but are forced to continue in a spiral movement. By the same token, when progressing beyond symbolizing the spatial and nonspatial through the positive and the negative, it is necessary to proceed to something that is of a still higher order than the spatial and nonspatial.

"Let us assume, then, that something exists that encompasses, that contains, both the spatial and the nonspatial, which is spatial and nonspatial at the same time. This requires the search for a third order. If in the realm of higher reality one really focusses upon the physically real, and one designates the physically real with a positive sign, then it becomes necessary to use a negative sign for the etheric, the real etheric. In the etheric one already leaves the spatial realm and enters the spiritual. If we wish to proceed into the astral, however, we can't get by with the spatial and the nonspatial; rather we must take into account a third element that has exactly the same relationship to the positive and the negative as in formal mathematics the imaginary numbers do to positive and negative numbers. And then, in moving from the astral to the entity of the 'I,' it would even be necessary to come up with a concept that would be superimaginary in relation to the concept of the imaginary. This is why I have always been so unsympathetic with the antipathy toward the superimaginary, because one really needs such a concept to ascend to the 'I.' It is impossible to leave it out. What is important is to apply it in the right way when remaining within purely formal mathematics; in order not to depart from reality, it is impossible to leave it out when proceeding correctly with mathematical formations so that one does not depart from reality.

"I discussed such a problem with someone I met today, and this problem clearly showed that even in mathematical operations there can be something that is exceedingly difficult to relate to reality; this is the problem of probabilities. In calculations for insurance, I can determine when someone will die. But this applies only to a crowd. It is impossible to conclude from this that a specific individual will die in the year that can be calculated. Reality thus falls outside my calculations. In the same way, it happens frequently that certain calculated results are formally correct but do not correspond to what is real. It could be, then, that the formal aspects of mathematics would occasionally have to be rectified in accordance with the results of superempirical reality. First it is necessary to prove whether it is correct that if $a \times b = 0$, one can only arrive at this result if one of the factors is 0. When one of the factors is 0, it is certainly true that one gets 0 as a result. But now the following question must be posed: is it possible that the result could be 0 if neither a nor b were 0? This could be the case if reality forced us to come to superimaginary (hypercomplex) numbers, which are then the corresponding correlates of a superempirical reality.

"Therefore mathematical work must be pursued to clarify the relationship of the real to the imaginary, and of the superimaginary to the imaginary and to the real. In order to do this, however, it could well be that it would become necessary to modify even the laws of calculating."

51. P.A.M. Dirac introduced superimaginary numbers into atomic physics for access to a deeper understanding of the electron. This step, in conjunction with the concepts of the quantum theory and the theory of relativity, created the possibility to think "anti-matter" within the thought forms of atomic physics. This "antimatter" is capable of destroying matter.

52. *William Preyer* (1841-1897). Physiologist and psychologist.

53. *Emil Du Bois-Reymond* (1818-1896). German physiologist. Rudolf Steiner frequently referred to his lecture, *Concerning the Boundaries of the Knowledge of Nature*, given in Leipzig on August 14, 1872.

54. The experiments that are described in Lecture XI but that were not completed at that time were demonstrated with a somewhat modified apparatus of which no sketch is available.

55. The exact quotation is, "The nearer the world process comes to equilibrium and the smaller the difference in intensity, the slower the progress toward equilibrium; with infinitely small differences it becomes infinitely slow. Thus the process does not completely cease in finite time, but it infinitely approaches equilibrium in finite time so that the infinitely long remainder, because of its infinitely small processes, can be disregarded. The principle of depreciation teaches us that the world process *is running down*

and that in finite time it must reach a stage where *no more energy transformations are possible*. This occurs long before the temperature differences become infinitely small" Eduard von Hartmann, *Grundriss der Naturphilosophie* (Bad Sachsa, 1907).

56. The sketch to which Steiner was referring here is not extant.

57. *Eugen Kolisko* (1893-1939). Teacher in the first Waldorf School in Stuttgart and author of natural scientific and medical literature. The title of his talk may have been, *A Chemistry Free of Hypotheses*.

58. A theory that attributed the electricity arising in a thunderstorm to the friction of steam against air was developed by Friedrich Jordan in a popular newspaper found in Rudolf Steiner's library. Jordan rejuvenates older views summarized in the *Grande Encyclopedie* (Paris, approximately 1896) in the article called, "Foudre" ("Lightning"): "The analogy between lightning and the electric spark was noted from the moment one was able to produce adequately strong sparks. This led to the assumption that conditions exist in the atmosphere similar to those that produce the electricity in our machines. The latter utilize the production of electricity by friction or by an influence of neighboring electrified bodies. The hypothesis of clouds being electrically charged by friction against mountain slopes or other clouds derives from this."

59. *Hermann von Baravalle* (1898-1973). Teacher at the Waldorf School in Stuttgart and later founder of Waldorf schools in the U.S.A. He published extensively in the fields of mathematics, physics, astronomy, and education. *Ernst Blümel* (1884-1952). Mathematician, teacher at the first Waldorf School in Stuttgart. *Alexander Strakosch* (1879-1958). Construction engineer. Taught at the Waldorf School in Stuttgart and became a member of the executive body for the Scientific Research Institute of *Der kommende Tag* in Stuttgart.

60. The spiritual or cultural life, the life of rights, and the economic life. In 1920 Rudolf Steiner was intensely involved in publicizing his ideas about the threefolding of the social organism. See his book, *The Threefold Social Order* (Anthroposophic Press, Spring Valley, NY).

61. A third natural scientific course took place in Stuttgart from January 1-18, 1921, The Astronomy Course, not yet available in English.

Addendum to notes for Lecture X:

There may be mention of the experiments in lectures given by Tyndall in the US 1872 - 1873 and published by the University of Adelaide, Australia as an epub. The website is
https://ebooks.adelaide.edu.au/t/tyndall/john/six-lectures-on-light/index.html (also available as Gutenberg item:http.gutenberg.org/files/14000/14000-h/14000-h.htm).

www.ingramcontent.com/pod-product-compliance
Lightning Source LLC
Chambersburg PA
CBHW020052170426
43199CB00009B/252